Music and the Dance

MUSIC AND THE DANCE

ELWOOD R. PRIESING

An Exposition-Banner Book

Exposition Press Hicksville, New York

First Edition

Inquiries should be addressed to Exposition Press, Inc., 900 South Oyster Bay Road, Hicksville, N.Y. 11801

Library of Congress Catalog Card Number: 77-84536

ISBN 0-682-48957-3

Printed in the United States of America

Contents

Preface

THE DANCE has been the foundation of so much music that musicians should know more about dance history. In order to play with greater understanding, we should know the story of such dances as the minuet, waltz, polka, tango, and others plus their general musical style as well as the costumes worn by the dancers.

The cultural traits of each race and age have been carried into its merrymaking. Costumes have also played their part in the evolution of the dance. Thus the minuet was the dance for an age of great formality and precise manners—for bewigged and perfumed courtiers, who had ample time to learn the graces of such a dance. What courtier would risk setting his or her powdered wig askew by dancing the frug, the samba, or the Charleston with its side kicks and contorted leg-twisting. These latter were dances for the short-skirted, short-haired, unencumbered dancers of the twentieth century.

Our great composers enjoyed the dances of their day. We constantly read how they improvised in dance forms; for improvising has always been a means for accompanying the dance.

Bach's interest in dance music must have caused him to write his suites. Haydn loved the Slavonic dances and tunes of his native Croatia; and, since he wrote for a court full of gaiety and dancing, he found it wise to incorporate the minuet and other formal dance tunes into his symphonies. Mozart was an accomplished dancer, whose wife stated that he often said it was dancing, not music, that he really cared for. The supposedly austere Brahms was fond of dance rhythms. In his youth he was well known for playing dances at balls and inns. He loved the Viennese waltzes of his day, and it is related that he played them so charmingly that one evening, after a dinner party, while all the guests were putting on their coats in the hall below, Brahms asked his host, "Shall I call them back?" Then, leaving the doors open, he sat down and played waltzes as only he could, until he had lured each guest back upstairs.

The entire development of musical style has been affected by dance rhythms, dance patterns, and the dance spirit. In the barbaric dances before the red glow of primitive fires, each step was accompanied by throbbing drums, and every stamp of foot and leap or shout was an accent. Our rhythmic patterns have developed from such beginnings, just as melody has evolved from the babble of the observers and the chants of the dancers.

Many of our dance compositions are not intended for dancing, although they are based on dance style, rhythm, and form. Thus we have the scherzi of Beethoven, the waltzes, mazurkas and polonaises of Chopin, and works of other composers who have sought to express the feelings associated with dancing, or to create fanciful and grotesque dances to which we can dance only in our imagination. Similarly, while the Strauss waltzes were intended for dancing, the "Hungarian Dances" of Brahms were his favorite Hungarian dance tunes arranged for pianists to play in their homes, while the "Hungarian Rhapsodies" of Liszt were collections of gypsy dance tunes arranged for the concert performances of virtuoso pianists. On the other hand we have such programmatic works as Liszt's "Mephisto Waltz," which is intended to describe an episode from Lenau's *Faust,* and von Weber's "Invitation to the Dance," as well as Saint-Saens's "Dance Macabre," which are based on the form of nineteenth-century concert waltzes.

Acknowledgments

This book represents a compilation and expansion of a series of articles printed in the *Junior Keynotes* magazine of the National Federation of Music Clubs for the benefit of music teachers and students. It seeks to reveal the colorful background of dance forms known to music lovers since the Middle Ages. It is a reduction of a much more comprehensive manuscript on the history of dance music.

Acknowledgments of appreciation must be given to the print libraries of the Metropolitan Museum of Art, particularly the Harris Brisbane Dick Fund, and the New York Public Library and especially to the latter's extensive divisions of music and the dance. Thanks must be expressed to Dr. Jack Sacher, musicologist at Montclair State College, for his valuable suggestions; to Howard Linn Edsall, for his encouragement; to Isabel Marting, who expressed her interest and enthusiasm from the inception of the writing of this book in the early days of the Dance Library and through the time of her appointment as librarian of the Juilliard School of Music; and to my wife, for her loyal support and assistance.

ELWOOD R. PRIESING

Introduction

The relationship of the dance to music has so often been discussed that it may be wise to describe it. Let us say that the dancer expresses his interpretation of music with bodily motions, as the singer uses his voice, and the violinist uses the violin.

Throughout dancing, several feelings exist: physical exuberance, emotional expression, desire for admiration, esthetic pleasure, religious veneration.

In primitive society, music and the dance were the natural expression for joy and abandon. Just as children whirl and jump in excitement, or shout and imitate the sounds about them, so primitive dancers skipped, hopped, jumped, and shouted for sheer ecstasy.

Many tribes believed that they learned to dance from the animals. Some Australian peoples danced a kangaroo dance wherein the men imitated the postures, leaps, and sounds of a kangaroo. Primitives frequently mimicked their victories of hunt and battle before the audience of admiring womenfolk.

In primeval times the dance was accompanied by such primitive sounds as the rhythmic beats of drums, shells, or even hands. Frequently grunts, simple songs, and chants were added. In the kangaroo dance, while the men performed their steps, the women accompanied by rhythmically knocking two pieces of wood together and singing a simple tune over and over.

In the second stage, dance became a part of religion. For primitives, dancing continued until the tribes reached a state of trance, which they felt made them almost godlike. The medicine man was a dancer, using the dance as a magical means of cure and prophecy. His people echoed his beliefs by dancing for magical success in health and harvest, as well as for pure enjoyment of movement. Such dancing was used to attain strength to overcome dangers. Each tribe found its own magical answer to thwart natural and human perils. However, the effort to thwart the evil spirits was not only for the magic, but for the fun.

Dancing assumed great importance in acts of worship among the American Indians. The term "dance" meant a ceremony which frequently continued for many days and included group dances, solo dances, recitations, and songs. The Aztecs omitted five days from their yearly calendar and devoted them to the dance. The snake dance of the Hopis was an elaborate ceremonial lasting for several days and was intended as an appeal for rain. In one part, live rattlesnakes were carried in the hands, and even held between the teeth, while the performers stamped and postured.

The third phase of the dance made it an art form, apart from religion, although it was religion which fostered this development. Now, temple dancers entered the courts of rulers, and man consciously changed the primitive abandon and added racial characteristics and personal expression to form dance patterns. Such dancing grew from an amateur art form into a specialized field for expression and technique. Eventually it became the means for the expression of ideas and dramatic spectacles. Dancers and ballet masters sought to tell stories, to express their ideas by pantomime. In time this produced our great ballet and dance spectacles, using music specially written by such great composers as Stravinsky, Ravel, Aaron Copland, and others.

The social dance is still another phase of dancing. This cannot actually be classified as an art, since it is often little more than a means to channel energy. If, however, a dancer seeks to bring order to this energy and wishes to make it state something, it becomes an art.

The social dance is peculiar to the Western World, for in the Orient and ancient nations, social life was entirely masculine. Women were kept in seclusion. Medieval Europe maintained this Oriental attitude toward women until about A.D. 1000, when a new freedom developed as the knightly troubadours were singing in sunny Provence. Here the dance became a means to enjoy social pleasures with the opposite sex.

True, men and women both danced from ancient times, but even in the primitive round, the sexes danced apart, and the women who danced formed a circle inside or outside that of the men.

The use of instruments for dance accompaniment was a later development. People used their voices before there were any instruments. The original time-beaters were the stamping foot and the clapping hands. Eventually dancers attached rattles to their ankles, knees, and arms. Finally more elaborate noise instruments appeared, such as slit drums, scrapers, and bell-like instruments.

In the festival dances of many American Indians, the steps corresponded to drum rhythms, while language controlled the rhythmic figures with the voice. The use of word repetition eventually developed into melodic repetition. Thus dance tunes probably originated as in the spirituals, where a biblical sentence is repeated over and over.

Only after the appearance of dance songs did the use of melodic instruments appear. This was not a development of the drum and rhythmic instruments, but of the dance song, for in all cultures people sang melodies before they had instruments. Melody composed for purely instrumental purposes was a later and higher development.

Thus we observe how the dance helped and stimulated musical growth.

Music and the Dance

1

Origins of the Spectacular Dance

THE SPECTACULAR DANCE is largely an outgrowth of sacred rites. Primitive man did not know the physical laws of nature. He did not understand rainfall, droughts, fire, earthquakes or night and day. He peopled the world with powerful gods and spirits, who controlled the forces of nature. To placate these gods, he felt it was essential to offer sacrifices and violent physical exertion. The dance offered the medium for this expression and seemingly possessed magic powers for inducing communion with the gods.

Anyone who has felt the ecstasy of dance movement can gain some understanding of how dancing carried the primitive out of self, intoxicated, loosened the bonds of everyday living, and transported the performer to a trancelike state of exhilaration and power.

Sometimes these dances use natural body motions to gain bliss and magic power, and, by the added assistance of ordered rhythm, dancers attain new heights of ecstasy. On the other hand, dancers can utilize motions against natural impulses. They twist and turn, throwing themselves into convulsive movements. Thus the medicine man twisted himself into such paroxysms that blood flowed from his nose and mouth. By this means he sought a trancelike state to communicate with the gods. Hindu girls who perform stylized ritual dances may actually feel a trembling ecstasy which overcomes them during the course of a dance.

Often the achievement of the magic trance is aided by the hypnotic effect of sounds. Dark vowel sounds such as "um-my-owe" are an example. The Veddic priest became possessed by reciting a charm over and over. Gradually he danced more and more quickly, and his voice became hoarser. Soon he became possessed by the

Yaku (spirit), and, although he did not become unconscious and could coordinate his movements, he had no clear memory of what he said, and only a general idea of his movements.

The superhuman power which accompanied such a condition seems unbelievable. In the ancient world, men became eunuch priests of a god. Ecstatic dancers of the Cappadocian Ma were lashed by the noise of drums until they gashed themselves and spilled their blood before an idol. The devil-possessed Negroes of the Sudan danced and circled until, at the climax of their emotional frenzy, they swallowed burning coals.

The cramped poses and contorted muscles of convulsive dances are often carried over into art dancing. Oriental girls are trained from early childhood how to twist the soft bones and joints of their arms and legs until they can move them in unnatural poses. In the "belly" dance, which exists throughout the Orient, girls achieve such control of their muscles that they can raise the plates of their abdomens up and down. In our modern dance and even in the ballet, we can see how our muscles can be trained to perform remarkable feats; we also observe some movements adopted from Oriental sources.

The medicine man was the agent who transformed the dance from frenzied movement into art. Primitives soon decided that a standardization of ceremonials was necessary if the ritual was to be successful. A priest who knew the gods and their whims was called upon to preserve and teach the tribe how to regulate the dances. Eventually such priests gained power; for, if tribal rites were unsuccessful, blame might be placed on a faulty performance, and penalties were meted out to performers who had made mistakes.

Rituals gradually became more complex, and a clan of priests and priest-actors emerged, who were trained in correct procedures. From such beginnings sprang the dancing master. The importance of his work occupied so much of his time, that he could not hunt or raise his crops. Eventually he received payment for his services of training the youth and preserving the rituals.

The evolution of religious rites into secular dance dramas has followed similar steps in each civilization. Almost every nation possesses some scene or myth which can be depicted by dance. Often these are elements of everyday life. The American Indian constantly repeated tales of the forest and victories in past battles. In Polynesia, the once-secret fraternity of Areoi adopted the practice of taking a series of dance dramas to the different islands. The strictly religious dances and pantomimes were followed by historical sketches, pantomimes, and comedy skits.

The ancient Egyptians crowded to see the priests reenact the life, death, and resurrection of Osiris with dance and song. The Holy Year commenced in August with the appearance of the star Sirius, regarded as the star of Isis. This was preceded by astronomic dances of the stars, performed in the hallowed secrecy of the temple by priests dressed in scintillating clothes and making signs of the Zodiac. Originally the choreography was plotted to follow the path of Sirius in order to determine when the dams of the Nile might be cut to release the flood waters. Other festivals followed throughout the year.

In ancient Greece, the people worshipped Dionysus, god of fertility, at festivals which developed into the great dramatic form of tragedy, which represented the fusion of all the elements of tribal rites, dancing, music, and poetry into the grand form of a danced drama.

The music and dancing of the high civilizations of the East were based on class differences produced by the conquest of nations. The upper class of conquerors did not work; hard labor was left to the second class, which also provided entertainment. The entertainers enjoyed a fairly high standing, and, through the practice of their art, the most beautiful and talented girls among the people gained the opportunity to live in comfort and even luxury, many becoming the wives and concubines of princes and wealthy traders.

In this art there was no definite boundary between music and the dance; entertainers were expected to be skillful in both.

Performers frequently formed a dynasty of their own, and, although men danced, the art was usually passed from mother to daughter. Girls were held in a sort of slavery and were often passed along singly or in groups, as a sort of ballet, from king to king or his favorite. Thus every court had many foreigners who imparted an exotic charm to entertainments and also produced an interchange of racial types and ideas. For instance, when the court of the Alhambra was at its zenith in Spain in 1400, many Oriental dancers were imported by the Moorish conquerors. Through them, Oriental styles penetrated into Europe and even into Germany, where they became a factor in Western music and dancing.

Thus we discern that the twin arts of music and the dance have been carried down through the ages by devoted practitioners from priest to dancing master and performer.

2

Dances of Medieval Nobility

SOCIAL DANCING with mingling of the sexes did not develop until after the year A.D. 1000. In the ancient world the men danced and the women danced, but they never danced together. The Church had long held that women should be silent. However, a new spirit of reverence toward the Virgin Mary came into being after the first thousand years. The first appearance of the new cult appeared by 1050 with the compositions of the first Mary hymns, the Ave Marias. Shortly after, the knightly troubadours evidenced a new deference toward their ladies.

The crusades brought about a great blending of cultures, and knights learned of different ways of life as they tramped through France and the fair land of Provence in the far southeast, near the golden courts of Moorish Spain. There, in castles built on craggy rocks, the knight appeared in the new guise of a devoted slave to the lady of his choice. He almost forgot his sword in order to compose poetry. Such knights were called troubadours (*trobar* is Provençal for "to find" or "to compose"). In northern France they were called *trouvères,* and in Germany, *Minnesingers.*

Eleanor of Aquitaine is credited with introducing the art to northern France when she became queen. She was the daughter of Guillaume IX, Duke of Aquitaine (1087-1127), the earliest troubadour whose works still exist. Eleanor initiated the famous "Courts of Love" wherein she and her ladies acted as judges, passing upon the merits of cases of love and, more important, upon the merits of the poetry of competing troubadours. The winning poet was crowned and the event celebrated by a banquet and ball.

Amid such poetic surroundings, where an increasingly gay and aristocratic society filled the castles and dallied in gentle relationships between the sexes, the social dance was rediscovered as a means for genteel pleasure. The first dances seem to have assumed a twofold aspect: there was a slow introductory dance processional usually accompanied by singing, then a gay dance characterized by leaping or skipping, performed as a couple dance with pairs of dancers accompanied by rebecs and stringed instruments.

Our term "carole" (from *corolla,* a little crown or garland) is derived from the introductory processional, which was a choral dance sung or "caroled" by the dancers. "Carole" means to dance in a ring to the accompaniment of song, although sometimes the carole appears to have become an extended line dance.

The carole dance spread rapidly throughout Europe. In Sweden it was first mentioned in 1260 as performed at a princely wedding. Youthful Danes studying at the University of Paris saw and joined in the carole dances before the Church of Our-Lady-of-the-Carole. Evidently this was a chain dance, a processional wherein the dancers turned from right to left with marching steps and beat one foot against the other. The choral leader, bearing either a glove, a bright flower, a cup, a May-branch, or at night a burning torch, led his company. In Italy, Giovanni Boccaccio mentioned the dance in his *Decameron* in 1353. Here, the story leader was elected queen of the group, and, attended by other ladies and two young men, she led off a stately carole to the music of a viol and a lute played by Dioneo (the pen name of Boccaccio himself).

The couple dance, which followed the carole, is a descendant of the sex motif of primitive fertility dances, although the dancing of the knights had little of the abandon of the peasants. Rather, it exemplified the three essentials of the service of love: joy, love, courtliness (*joi, amor, cortezia*).

One of the most elaborate descriptions of the twin forms of medieval dancing appears in the famous French poem "Le Roman de la Rose," written in about 1237 by Guillaume de Loris and translated into English verse by Chaucer before 1372. It describes an introductory procession accompanied by the sweet high tones of a girl singer; then men and maids trod their measures on the grass while "*minstrales*" and "*jonglours*" sang and played on flute and tambourine; next two damsels leaped forth, turned, embraced, and lithely swayed in graceful dance.

From the carollers' practice of circling about a leader who led

A Carole, *from a manuscript of "The Romance of the Rose"*

them in song have sprung many poetic forms, as songs were the musical accompaniment to aristocratic dancing. In them the leader sang one or two lines of poetry, and the chorus added a refrain, often accompanied by clapping. There are three forms of the troubadour dance-songs; the *rondeau, virelai,* and the *ballada.* The rondeau was the simplest form and must not be confused with the musical *rondo* of later times.

The earliest version was a poem with a six-line text divided into two musical units. These short units supplied all the musical material for the leader and the answering refrain of the chorus. In the following eight-line rondeau of Adam de la Halle, we note the refrain at the beginning and the end.

Rondeau of Adam de la Hale. This is Pierre Aubry's version, which appeared in an article "Refrains et Rondeaux du XIII Siècle," in Riemann's Festschrift *(Leipzig, 1909).*

Virelai ("Ce fut en Mai"), Moniot d'Arras

The virelai and the ballada used variations of the form of the rondeau. The name virelai may preserve the dance origin since the verb *virer* means "to turn around," and *lai* refers to a secular version of a sequence.

The Provençal ballada must not be confused with the Italian *ballata* or the English ballad, which is a narrative poem. True, all terms originated in the Latin *balare,* meaning "to dance," and referred to something which was sung and danced, for both arts were indispensable to each other. We quote herewith the best known early ballada, dating from the middle of the thirteenth century. Note the subtle changes in the meaning of the choral refrain in this tale of a coquettish "queen" who delights in the dance.

The poetical divisions of these dance-songs bear names connected with dance movements. Thus, when we say they sang or played a verse, the term meant they had reached the *versus,* or

Ballada ("A l'entrada del tems clar")

turning point, where dancers joined hands and danced their parts until they reached their original starting point. Here, they either stopped altogether or started over again. Similarly, the parts of the *cantilenas* bore names of body movements. Thus, a *pes versus* would mean a turned foot.

The music of the medieval dance was a chantlike song, a rather monotonous repetition of catchy phrases. The tunes may have been derived from melodies which the troubadours heard in church, for there was no sharp line between sacred and secular music, and the adaptation of a love poem to a liturgical melody was quite acceptable. The troubadours accompanied the dancing by singing their own songs, but they never degraded themselves by playing an instrumental accompaniment. There seems to have been a taint clinging to the performance upon a musical instrument. A *jongleur* was called to supply such music. The Provençal term *joglar* reveals the kinship of such musicians to the juggler.

Jongleurs began to appear in the ninth century and may have been descendants of the Latin mime. Some jongleurs who were of a more cultured nature were invited to perform for good society, and a few even gave up wandering and took up service in feudal households, where they were classified as servants. Indeed, the French jongleur was called a *ménestrel,* from the Latin *minister* (inferior). His accomplishments included the ability to play some instrument, usually of the bowed family, such as the vielle, harp, lute, psaltery or a small portable organ. We do not know how these accompanied vocal music since the existing manuscripts are only one-line compositions. We do know that they accompanied dancing.

Italy was profoundly affected by the Italian visits of such troubadours as Raimbout de Vaquieras and the influence of Provence was clearly indicated in 1260 when the Florentine poet Folgore da San Genignano wrote that, when the young men go forth in April, "ladies shall go with them to ride, display French dresses, dance Provençal figures or touch new instruments from Germany." For the Provençal dance-songs became the heirlooms of the Italians.

A vast number of compositions by poets were in existence by the fifteenth century, and lyrics with accompanying music and caroles were performed for such festivities as May morning tournaments, carnival processions, banquets, and summer evening dances on the piazzas of Florence. An entire set of thirteenth- and fourteenth-century dance melodies was published in 1907 by Pierre Aubry and Johannes Wolf. These include *stantipes, estampies,* and *danses royales.* Of these, little or nothing is known about the performance of the *danses royales,* which resembled the *estampie* in their form of four movements with the same refrain.

The *estampie* is the oldest known type of medieval instrumental dance music. Originating in Provence as an *estampida,* called *estampita* in Italy, and *estampie* in France, they were fiddled by the jongleurs on their vielles as accompaniment to the gliding of the nobility. The fourteenth-century theorist Johannes Grocheo wrote that an *estampie* was a "melody without words composed from a succession of *puncta,* or melodic periods, each of which was a little dance by itself with symmetrical phrases." Other authorities add that the *puncta* had the same principle as the return dance, wherein the performers took a few steps forwards, then returned to the starting point.

Evidently the *estampie* was once of a stamping nature, if we trace the word to the Frankish *stampon.* However, the musical form seems to be derived from the *stantipes* of the Italian ballata, where the terms *stantipes* and *ductia* referred to the instrumental offshoots of the form. Grocheo adds that the *estampies* and *ductia* were so difficult that they "absorbed the minds of youths and maidens" preventing evil thoughts, while the *ductia* even had "power over the passion called 'love.'"

The British Museum possesses fifteen one-line Italian dance melodies, apparently written for the vielle. They include eight *estampies,* one *trotto* and six *saltarelli,* a name which indicates a jumped or leaped dance, since *sault* means jump. Five of the *saltarelli* are in triple time and the other, in duple time, is a German *saltarello* or *quaternaria.* The *trotto* in the manuscript apparently represents a dance in which the feet were vigorously set down. Since this appears with the *saltarelli,* which were stepped, evidently certain dances had a sort of trotting step.

The evolution of such instrumental dance forms reflects the growing complexity of dance and song. With the growth of the musical *punctus* from eight to sixteen bars of music and the increasingly complex polyphonic structure, it became essential to use instruments for all dance accompaniments.

By the middle of the fourteenth century, the art of the gallant French *trouvère* had greatly changed, and the old courtly chivalry existed only as a literary flourish. Now for the first time, a purely musical form develops from the dance, as the rondel becomes a poem, and the rondeau changes from a poem for dancing into a purely instrumental form in contrapuntal style.

3

The Dance of Death

FOR THOUSANDS OF YEARS it has been the custom to link the approach of winter with death. Similarly, Halloween is now associated with grinning pumpkin faces, masked beggars, and the dance of skeletons rising from the grave, an idea which was musically depicted by Saint-Saens in his famous orchestral composition "Dance Macabre."

In primitive cultures, tribes circled about a corpse to protect both dead and living from hostile spirits. Masked men danced around, and a masked medicine man led the rites. The people of the Stone Age depicted gruesome pictures of the *dance of death*. In Italy an early Greek tomb portrays three corpses dancing. The dance of death is a feature of religions founded on ancestor worship, where such dancing was thought to induce a closer union with the dead. In China the dance was performed to enable the soul of the deceased to find his ancestors.

In ancient Rome, the early Christians met in the catacombs where they held religious services on the tombs of martyrs whose bodies had been rescued from the Roman Arena. Later, the altars of many cathedrals and churches were built with a cavity or sepulcher to hold the bones and relics of a martyr in order to remind the congregations of the similar death and resurrection of Christ after his martyrdom. Even the altar of St. Peter's Cathedral in Rome was built over the tomb of the apostle. And the actions of priests at Holy Communion might seem a reflection of ancient rites.

In the Middle Ages, the churchyard with its ghostlike tombs and shadows was deemed the proper place for people to dance when they wished to assuage the dead whom they might join at any time. Pictures of the dance of death depict movements and grotesque representations of whirling skeletons. The fleshless, clattering bones

Dance of the Dead, *from Hartmann Schedel's* Weltchronik, *Nürnberg, 1493*

reflect the primitive elements of the medieval mind and seem an echo of the masks and mummery of ancient vegetation rites.

Although the origins of the European dance of death are hidden in obscurity, the idea seems to have spread from the Orient, perhaps brought from the Moorish civilization of Spain, the source of so much medieval song and dance. From here came our word *macabre,* for the Arab word for grave is *quabre* or *Kabr,* while the *makbaba* is a cemetery. Furthermore, the later medieval concept about life—that all are equal before death, make good use of your life—seems very similar to that of the ancient Arabian warning couplet that appears above the gates of many Arabian graveyards:

> As you are, so were we;
> We are what you shall be.

This idea is also echoed in the earliest surviving music of a dance of death, which was found in a fourteenth-century manuscript in the mountain monastery of Montserrat, near Barcelona, Spain. Here it was included among a number of pilgrim songs intended to be sung and danced by pilgrims on their way to the shrines of Spain.

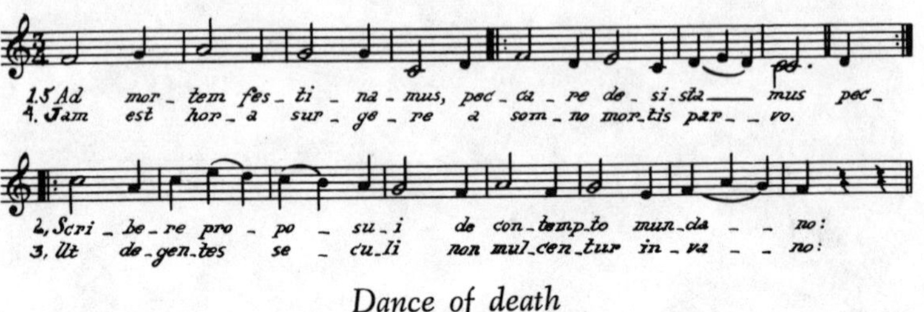

Dance of death

"We hurry toward death; let us desist from sin. I have resolved to write concerning contempt of the earth, so that the living of the world may not be cursed in vain. Now is the hour to rise from the evil sleep of Death."

There are many other stories about the dance of death and the various aspects of it in history.

* * *

The outbreak of the Hundred Years' War in 1337, followed ten years later by the scourge of the plague of the black death, occurred near the end of the era of faith known as the Middle Ages.

The climax of the plague was accompanied by dance manias which began in the East and spread to Germany and then westward. In 1347, a group of men and women danced through Belgium and Holland. It is said that as many as eleven hundred persons were included, since even onlookers were affected, being impelled to dance until they fell down. The famous tale of the Pied Piper of Hamlin, who lured the children by his magical piping, dates from this period. So also must the Italian *tarantella,* a dance in which humans, bitten by the poisonous tarantula spider, whirled until exhaustion to rid themselves of the deadly poison.

The bubonic plague, or black death, which struck all ages and ranks of society, vividly brought to prominence the concept that all are equal before death. The idea is mirrored in all the arts of the era. In paintings of the Last Judgment, we see Christ assigning souls to heaven and hell, and we see popes and mitered bishops among the damned, as well as soldiers, workmen, and housewives. In many pictures, the dance of death shows a round dance for men, only with the leader personified as a horrible apparition of Death. These grotesque distortions of the period are reflected in the gargoyles perched upon Gothic cathedrals. In woodcuts, the skeletal specter of Death steals up behind mortals to snatch them from their pleasures.

Our illustration, the *Feast of Herod,* by Von Behem (1500-1550), shows the skeletal figure of Death with his hourglass approaching one couple, and above Death is a procession bearing the head of John the Baptist to the dining table. The actions of the dancers are most interesting and varied. Some perform in rounds, others in couples. We should also note the type of instruments.

By the fifteenth century, the courts and society began to regale themselves more and more with masked entertainments. In England, the *morris dance* with its varied characters appeared in the time of Chaucer. Sometimes masked performers presented a play called a *mommerie,* a word taken from the Greek *momme,* meaning a mask.

The mummers were customarily silent, a custom which may have stemmed from primitive death rites, for funerals and anniversaries were once celebrated by banquets eaten in silence by masked humans. The mask also comes from ancient cultures in which masked dancing was thought to charm or alarm the spirits. In Roman funerals, maskers had represented the dead.

But, as Christian ideas permeated society, the old rites lost their meanings and became more like games. However, the peasants never ceased to feel that such games were somehow magical.

Fest der Herodias of Hans Sebald von Behem, 1530. *This half of the picture reveals dance motions typical of the time. Observe the skeletel figure of Death and the head of John the Baptist—also, the instruments accompanying the dancing.*

4

Masked Dances in the Middle Ages, the Moresca, and the Morris Dance

Masked Dances in the Middle Ages

There were several types of masked dances and mumming in the Middle Ages. Eventually these developed into the court masque and dramatic performances. These were: 1. the king-game and customs connected with the election of a mock ruler; 2. the *moresque* and *sword dances,* which included mimic combat or dance using costumed performers dressed to represent certain characters; and 3. mumming, where processions of people disguised by masks, beast-heads, or merely with discolored faces paraded in the streets or entered into neighbors' houses.

One of the earliest examples of such mumming is the Feast of Fools, first described in twelfth-century France. In this New Year's festival, the lower clergy took precedence above their superiors after electing one of their number to preside as Bishop (Pope or Abbot) of Fools. They celebrated with drinking bouts, riotous masquerading in beast-heads or women's clothing; they danced in the choir of the cathedral dressed as minstrels, panders, or women, sang wanton songs, and made fun of the divine offices by playing dice on the altar and swinging puddings and sausages instead of censers.

By the fifteenth century this travesty of religion was modified, but the Feast of Fools did not altogether die, and ordinary citizens adopted it. All over France, guilds of clerks, craftsmen, and students sprang up with *sociétés joyeuses,* who dressed in fools' dress and elected a leader as *Prince des Sots, Abbé des Fous,* and so forth. They amused themselves by burlesques, civic pageantry, and even playacting (*mystères mimes*).

In England, a Lord of Misrule was elected, who, accompanied by the "wilde-heds" of the parish, dressed in bright colors and, attended by hobbyhorses and pipers, disturbed the parsons by dancing through and around the church to the amusement of the congregation in general.

However, mumming by the lower classes was frequently prohibited in England, although there was little objection to the elaborate mumming of the nobility. Thus, in 1377 the commons of London visited Richard II as follows:

> For upon ye monday next before ye purification of our Lady at night, and in ye night were 130 men disguizedly apparailed and well mounted on horseback to goe on mumming to ye said prince, riding from Newgate through Cheape whear many people saw them with great noyse of trumpets, cornets and shawmes and great plenty of waxe torches lighted, and in the beginning they rid 48 after ye maner of esquiers two and two together clothed in cotes and clokes of red say or sendall and their faces covered with vizards well and handsomely made. . . . Finally ye prince caused to bring ye wyne and they dronk with great joye, commanding ye minstrels to play, and ye trompets began to sound and other instruments to pipe &c. And ye prince and ye lordes dansed on ye one syde, and ye mummers on ye other a great while and then they drank and took their leave and so departed toward London.*

It is interesting that this report makes no mention of women. We wonder if the ladies of the court joined in the dancing. It is more than likely that they did not, for women still led a restricted life, and on the occasion of the mumming before Richard II women probably did not dance with the mummers; they may not have been present.

The Moresca

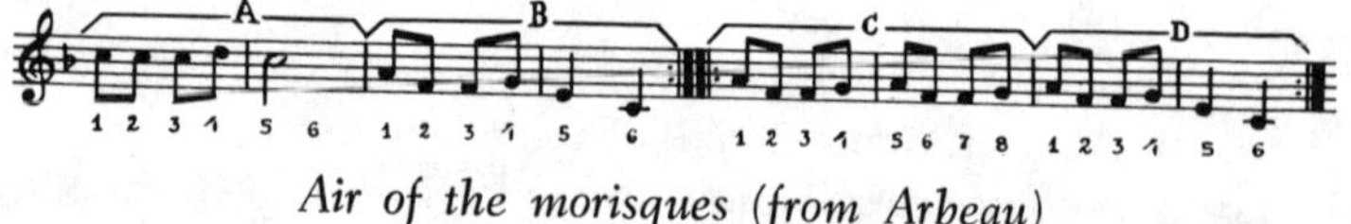

Air of the morisques (from Arbeau)

---

*From the "Harleian Manuscript."

The European version of the *morris dance,* the *moresca,* was performed by dancers with blackened faces. The moresca appeared all over Europe for at least three centuries. East Germans misspelled it *Moriska,* as if it were Polish. Spaniards called it *morisco,* and the Italians, *moresca.*

The dance was most appropriate in an era which delighted in masquerades, and it may hide an ancient fertility rite under the Moorish name, for the dance goes back further than the Moors, and versions appear all over Europe under similar disguises. Sometimes the sword is the connection with the fertility rite. In England we might observe that one performer has a hobbyhorse tied round his hips; of course, the horse is a fertility demon to many peoples. The Javanese had a hobbyhorse dance, and so did the Rumanians and Bulgarians. Even the ancient Greeks pictured horse dances on vases.

To go back further, the moresca was often performed in the spring, like the rites of Dionysus, where the leader had a blackened face as a symbol of winter, the dark season. The leader was beheaded in the course of the dance, or rather he appeared to be, while he hid behind the other dancers and lost his black face. Often at the end, he was raised on a shield or on joined swords. Thus we have many of the elements of a fertility rite in the morris dance.

The contrast of white and dark in the dance suggests the conflicts of the Europeans with the Moors or darker races of the East. This struggle later became a feature of the early ballets, which were characterized by fights between white- and dark-faced dancers. Perhaps this feature continued, because, after the Moors were expelled from Spain, the grandees retained Moslems for dances, which were performed with much tapping of feet and the tinkling of bells attached to the ankles. This Oriental color proved so attractive to Europeans that it was widely imitated.

In time it became connected with all types of bizarre dancing, and many undescribed dances of Europe came under the name moresca, some being pure inventions of dancing masters. Eventually the name was all that seems to have remained of the original dance, and it referred to a bizarre type of spectacular dance performed in costume. Included among these is the moresca which concludes Monteverdi's opera *L'Orfeo,* which is written in rapid

6/8, whereas those in 4/4 or 2/4 are associated with a more stately and processional type of dance.

The Morris Dance

For long it was incorrectly believed that the English morris dance had no connection with the continental moresca, but research indicates that the dance was brought to the island during the reign of Edward III (1327-77) by his son, John of Gaunt, who was noted for his fondness for wandering minstrels.

Further connection is verified by a tune printed in England in 1550, as a morris dance, and a tune for a moresque, printed by

Arbeau in France in 1588. The morris men performed on occasions of public rejoicing, and the dance was associated with Christian holidays as well as such events as coronations. In May, morris dancers circled about a maypole garlanded with "laylocks and golden chains." Sometimes the maypole would remain in position for a week, and every morning the morris men would dance about it for luck.

The performance usually required six men, selected for qualities such as agility. They appeared wearing costumes gay with bright-colored ribbons, rosettes, flowers, and greenery. The most important feature was pads of bells, tuned in musical intervals and worn on the legs.

Attending the six men were various personages who seem representative of English legendry from the time of the troubadours. There were a fiddler, a fool, and a ragman (who looked after the discarded clothing of the dancers). In addition there might be a treasurer, a cake-bearer, a sword-bearer, a moll, or a king and queen.

When the dance became associated with the month of May, a lady of the May was added. Sometimes the saga of Robin Hood was portrayed, and then the dancers included the outlaw, Maid Marian, Friar Tuck and Little John (played by a boy). Also there might be four whifflers, or marshals, the hobbyhorse, and a dragon. The most important of all characters was the fool, often called the "squire" or "Rodney." He acted as leader or master of ceremonies, and was usually one of the best dancers.

The morris required highly coordinated motions of foot, hand, and body to perform its complex rhythms. Sometimes a jig or solo dance was performed in addition to the set dances of the team, or side, which stood in two files with three men on a side. The dignified movements were performed with a grave restraint which is suggestive of ritualistic significance.

Originally the musical accompaniment was performed by the ancient combination of the pipe and tabor (a small drum). When these gave way to the fiddle, many old morris men are said to have stopped dancing, since they found themselves unable to dance with it, probably because they missed the rhythmic support of the drum.

Cecil Sharp collected many morris tunes, most of more recent date and composed for the fiddle. The old pipe tunes seem to have disappeared. One of the best-known morris tunes is "Country Gardens," named after its words which have no connection with the dance, but, like many other dance tunes, was probably selected by performers who liked the tune.

> Old woman, if you please,
> Will you come along with me
> Into my fine country gardens?

Most morris tunes are in 2/4 or 4/4 time.

The English morris dance seems to have been an offspring of ancient troubadour customs or even earlier pagan fertility rites. In some English villages, the procession of morris dancers was headed by a man carrying a sword upon which was impaled a cake decorated with flowers and ribbons. At Kirtlington, a lamb was carried, and at Kidlington, a lamb's skin. We quote a passage from Blount's *Ancient Tenures:*

> At Kidlington in Oxfordshire, the custom is, that on Monday after Whitson week, there is a fat live lamb provided, and that maids of the Town, having their thumbs ty'd behind them, run after it, and she that with her mouth takes and holds the lamb, is declared Lady of the Lamb, which, being dress'd with the skin hanging on, is carried on a long Pole before the Lady and her Companions to the Green, attended with Music and a Morisco dance of Men, and another of Women, where the rest of the day is spent in dancing, mirth and merry glee. The next day the lamb is part bak'd, boyl'd and rost, for the Ladies feast, where she sits majestically at the upper end of the Table, and her companions with her with music and other attendants, which ends the solemnity.

This particular feast, held in eighteenth-century England, is not the only example of a link between the morris dance and pagan rites, for we must not forget the appearance of the maypole, which seems to have come from druidic times.

The *canary* was a favorite dance in fifteenth-century *mascarades* and it seems singularly appropriate to the period when the great discoveries and explorations of America and the exotic East fired imaginations. Arbeau wrote:

> Some say this dance is common in the Canary Isles. Others, perhaps more correctly, assert it was derived from a ballet composed for a masquerade in which the dancers were dressed as kings and queens of Mauretania, or else like savages in feathers dyed in many hues.

The English thought the dance originated in Spain where it was danced with castanets. According to Arbeau, the partners stood at opposite sides of a room and danced toward each other and back again, while executing steps as strange and bizarre as possible, "such as savages use." The dance must have been highly entertaining to youths who could improvise steps to their hearts' content.

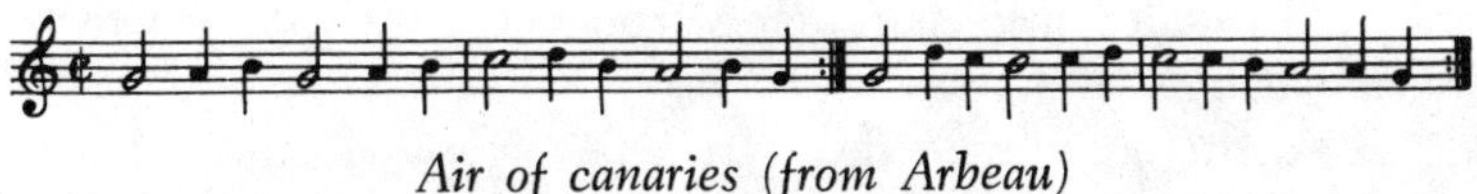

Air of canaries (from Arbeau)

Canaries (from Couperin, Book I, Ordre 2)

The music was originally chanted and was 2/2 meter. Later, in his *Dictionary of Music* (1768), J. J. Rousseau noted that the canaries of his day were somewhat similar to the gigues, being written in quick 3/8, 6/8, and even 6/16 meter. The tune always began on the first beat of the measure and was distinctive for the dotted first beat. It was composed in two-part form with each part repeated.

In England the dance was performed to practically the same music as the dance called the *hay;* some Elizabethan compositions being marked for either dance.

Lully and Purcell used the canary in their operas; Couperin included one in the second ordre of his *Clavecin Pièces, Book 1.*

5

The First Dancing Masters

SOCIAL DANCING became an art in fifteenth-century Renaissance Italy. Allied to it was an art of perfect social behavior, wherein carefully trained men and women conducted life's daily activities with a mannered grace.

To assist in learning these arts, the profession of the dancing master came into being. His primary purpose was to teach dancing, but he also trained his pupils in social etiquette.

Until now, the professional dancer had been a despised juggler or a wandering mime. People had danced from mere elation, learning from participation or simple observation. But with the Renaissance, the dancing teacher achieved great prestige in aristocratic circles, especially in northern Italy, where he enjoyed high social rank and was the companion of princes. In Venice, the dancing master even took the place of the bride's father in the silent dance which presented the bride before a wedding.

Along with this came the beginning of dance theory, and some dance masters are still known for articles which they wrote. Among these were Antonio Cornazano (about 1431-1515), Giovanni Ambrosio, and Guglielmo Ebreo (born 1440). All served the House of Sforza in Milan. All were influenced by Domenico da Ferrara, who seems to have founded a very distinct school of dancing by the middle of the fifteenth century.

The dances of this aristocracy had little heavy stamping, high leaps, or vigorous clasping and swinging of partners in circles and interweaving lines. True, certain types of peasant step and movement were adopted by the nobles, but these were adapted. For lords and ladies had long hours of leisure which could be devoted to the cultivation of subtle refinements, with a precision of step and body which were acquired only after considerable training.

Clothing itself played a part in restraining the movements of the dancers; for a long train trailing up to five yards of heavy material prevented rapid whirling. Furthermore, the long, pointed shoes worn by men, and the short doublet with tight fitting hose, though they may have looked comfortable, were actually so very tight that it was said that men had to be sewn into their clothing in the morning.

Renaissance dancers did not hold hands; the gentleman merely touched his lady's extended fingertips as she walked with lowered eyes and a beautiful smile, executing her paces in a stately and dignified fashion, gracefully turning and undulating her upper body from the hips.

The principal dances of society, the *basse danses* and the *balli,* were planned in purely formal lines by dancing masters. In this they followed the general trends of the day toward conducting life's activities in a more polite manner.

Most dance treatises begin with a theoretical explanation of terms and movements, followed by directions for performing specific dances composed by the dancing master and usually accompanied by dance tunes. Sometimes, the treatises contain artistic theories regarding dancing.

These aristocratic dances were elaborate and highly conventionalized. They were based on sequences of steps soon to be transported all over Europe and known by the abbreviations of their names, as follows:

s-simple
ss-two simples
d-double
R-reverence or bow
r-ripress
c-continuenza (in Italy) and congé (in France), a leave-taking.

These steps might be listed under the music in the following manner:

R b ss ddd r b c

This indicates the following steps: reverence, branle, two simples, three doubles, ripress, branle, congé. The arrangements for such a succession of steps varied according to the wishes of the dance master and required definite length of time which was precisely noted in the music by Italians and French.

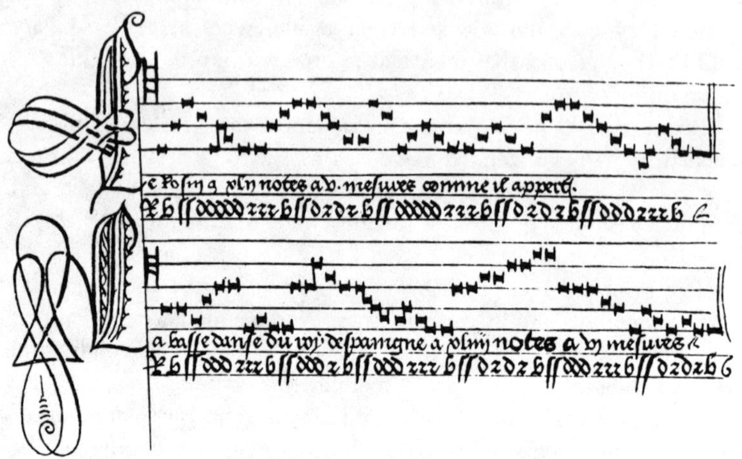

From manuscript "Basse Danses of Marguerite d'Autriche," circa 1450. Courtesy Dance Collection, the New York Public Library at Lincoln Center, Astor, Lenox and Tilden Foundations

The above illustration is from a treasured manuscript known as the "Basse Danses de Marguerite d'Autriche." The beautiful booklet, made of heavy black parchment, was inscribed in glittering gold and silver for the princess, a daughter of the Emperor Maximilian. Observe that the dance notation is beneath the notes. This music is not a tune, but the foundation melody, called a "tenor" or *cantus firmus,* upon which musicians were expected to improvise counterpoint for two or more voices or instruments.

If performed by instruments, the tenor was played by a slide trumpet which could be clearly heard blowing single tones of the theme in strictly even time, to which the dancers had to fit their step units, whether these be a double, two simples, or others. Accompanying the trumpet were often two or three shawms, which had a nasal timbre like an oboe. Also, chords might be played on the crossflute accompanied by a simple melody on the lute, and assisted by the drum.

The dancing master Giovanni Ambrosio suggested that instead of all instruments playing as an ensemble, each play alone: "the pifare will play one air, the organi will play one air, the harp another air and the tamburino still another." Apparently this implies contrapuntal improvisation over the tenor. Meanwhile, the dancer attempted to perform steps with each instrument, for, "If he cannot adapt his movements to the air, the measure and tempo of each, his dancing will be imperfect and it will be a sign that he does not understand."

The simple and double steps have been well described by sixteenth-century masters such as Arbeau. Thus, in the simple, to the time value of two bars, the left foot moved slightly forward; the other was drawn after it. In the double, during the time value of four bars: 1. step out with the left foot; 2. slide the right past it; 3. slide the left past; 4. stand.

Unfortunately, the terms are not complete enough for us to reproduce the dance, for the aristocrats knew the steps from practice and only had to memorize their order, as arranged by the dance master. Apparently most dancers used much more body action than we might realize. Often they contained steps derived from fencing. Guglielmo Ebreo writes of swaying movements of the body described as *aiero,* a certain swaying and upward movement of the body with a corresponding settling down. This may indicate a sway from the hips, recalling the protruding hip of the Gothic period. The *scossetto* meant a slight trembling, while *movemento* indicated a general movement, especially a rhythmical bending of hips, knees and ankles. Dancers also rose up and down on their toes. All these motions gave added motion to the generally slow *basse danse.*

Arbeau

In 1588, one of the most valuable books about the dance appeared, the famous *Orchesography,* by the Frenchman Thoinot Arbeau (1519-1595). Although the book was printed when Arbeau was sixty-nine, it is valuable, since it describes the dances of his youth. Arbeau is most interesting, having been a French monk and a cathedral canon who transposed his real name of Jehann Tabouret. He is, perhaps, the first person to give detailed descriptions of dances, along with the actual tunes to which the steps and motions fitted. He describes the ballroom dances of his day to an imaginary pupil, Capriol, to whom he also explains the proper conduct of a young man in society. As our illustration reveals, quaint pictures illustrate the steps, and Arbeau includes the rhythm of the tambour or drum, which he says is essential for the dancers.

The music for the dances is printed on the treble clef, and represents actual tunes of a folklike quality with words, even as in the present. Arbeau uses definite four-measure phrases, revealing that dancers followed tunes rather than music designed to fill out the patterns laid out by a dance master. It is interesting that, during this period, the first printed music for the dance appeared, one of the publishers being the French printer Attaignant.

Another, but less thorough, book on the dance was printed as early as 1536, by Antonius Arena in France, for by now France was becoming a leader in the dance, perhaps due to the interest of the famous Italian Queen of France, Catherine de Medici. Among other dances, Arena discusses the contemporary basse dance and the *branle.*

The *basse danse* was the most famous dance for aristocratic society in the Renaissance. In truth, we might call this the age of the *basse danse.* In it, dancers stepped or paced the measures without the hops and leaps of the lively high-stepped *danses hautes* of the country folk. Hence, the adjective *bassa* (low).

The *basse danse* first appeared in about 1400 and was in vogue until about 1550. Differing from other dances of the time, it had no prescribed order of steps. Its movements depended upon the ingenuity of the dancing master, who strung together bows, simple and double steps, turns and oscillations of the body. Any number of dancers might participate. Sometimes the masters called for two, three, or four performers who proceeded in couples or in a chain (*alla filia*). Also, trios composed of two men and a woman, or two women and a man seem to have been popular.

During the one hundred and fifty years of its popularity, there were many changes in its performance. Before 1450, there were only dances devised by dancing masters, bearing separate names. By 1500, the individual names were patterned on such terms as *basse danse majeur, basse danse mineur*. Finally, by 1550, this was narrowed further, and the special script devised by a dancing master was not used.

In its earlier period, the *basse danse,* like the carole and other medieval dances began with a pantomime and was followed by two contrasting dances. These were a sort of slow, processional type of dance (*basse danse majeur*) followed by a lively leaping type of dance, called a *saltarello*. Finally the performance concluded with a shorter dance termed the *basse danse mineur,* which was half as long as the first and was called by Arbeau the *retour de la basse danse*. However, by Arbeau's time, it became customary to dance the shorter *basse danse* after the first and to place the saltarello at the end.

The *saltarello* bore different names in various countries. Because the feet left the ground, Spaniards called it a high dance (*alta danza*) and Germans called it *Springdantze*. Yet, despite the fact that *sault* means leap, the dance was seldom a leaping dance; indeed by the fifteenth century it was not fashionable for good dancers to leap off the ground. Instead there was a slow rising and dropping on the toes.

The unity of the *basse danse* and the saltarello was so customary that the music of the second dance was usually a rhythmic variation of the first. Often the second dance was not written, since the musician was expected to transpose the saltarello from the music of the *basse danse*. However, it was played nearly twice as fast.

According to Arbeau the *basse danse* was very slow with three beats to the measure. He gives definite instructions for the entire performance including definite directions for playing the drum beats on the tambour or tabor.

A brief description of the performance of a basset, or *basse danse,* is written by Castiglione in his *Il Cortegiano,* in the early years of the sixteenth century: "My lady Duchesa desired Madonna Margarita and Madonna Costanza Fregosa to dance. Whereupon Barletti, a very charming musician and an excellent dancer, who always kept the court in good humor, began to play upon his instruments, and joining hands, the ladies danced first a basset and then a roegarse with consummate grace to the great delight of those who saw them."

The *roegarse* was in this case the after-dance of the *basset.* In certain areas it took the place of the customary saltarello. It was a folk dance from the French town of Rouergue, south of Lyons, which had been adapted for aristocratic performance. It did not have long popularity. Arbeau advises that the *tourdion* was the dance which replaced the saltarello.

In time the *pavane* replaced the *basse danse.* Arbeau indicates that at first it may have preceded the *basse danse.* Possibly it was used for the customary processional which preceded dances.

The Ballo

Aside from the standard dances about which Italian dance masters, assuming everyone knew them, give so little information, there was another type of dance composed by dance masters for the aristocracy. These were the balli, which were so frequently described by later writers like Caroso and Negri.

A ballo was an irregular type of dance. Differing from the *bassa danzas,* the balli were dance pantomimes: each bore a special name which usually indicated the topic of the pantomime. However, although they bore the aspects of pantomimes, they were never acted out, and no realistic gesture or play of features occurred. All that appeared, besides the suggestive title, was a bare succession of choreographic figures which followed the outline of the plot. The courtship motif naturally appeared frequently. Thus in La Sobria, there is the favorite trio group of the period: one woman between two men, with the woman favoring one man. Sometimes three women and two men form a chain; the ladies go in the center, a saltarello commences and then, after a halt, comes an interplay of circling and changing places.

The inclusion of a saltarello may seem surprising. However, certain recurring directions indicate that such popular dances as the *piva, saltarello* and *quaternaria* provided the framework for the balli.

The music of the balli was characteristically different from the *basse danses.* Its meter frequently changed as if to indicate the type of dance included within the frame, whether this was a piva, saltarello, or other dance. Later musical suites seem to have continued this practice and had dances with varied changes in rhythm. Along with the advent of the *ballo,* dance composers began the practice of placing the melodies in the treble, although it is true that Guglielmo Ebreo required his dance tune composer to invent a tenor for his balli as well as for his *bassa danza.*

The practice of naming dances for their pantomimic content was eventually carried into music not intended for dancing, but which has certain suggestive implications. Thus many dances of the early suites of French composers like Chambonnières bore descriptive titles. The practice was continued in the suites of Couperin and still continues.

In the Renaissance, the compositions for dance orchestras show great diversity. Almost all groups and families of instruments were used; however the choice of such instruments was not left at random, for various kinds of dances differed not only in tempo, measure and step, but also in instrumentation. Thus the *basse danse* uses shawms and trumpet; the moresque used pipes and tabor; the chronicler Molinet even mentions a special style of tabor playing.

The most valuable evidences for the choice of instruments are the paintings on the richly decorated wedding chests in which a bride's dowry was placed. Often these depicted a wedding dance on the streets of Florence. Our picture shows five couples of a wedding party dancing the much-loved wedding dance of the early Renaissance, the *chiarenzaro,* under a baldachin with the Baptistry of Florence in the background. The bride's headgear of peacock feathers identifies the newlyweds as the last couple. The musicians,

Italian painted chest, fifteenth century

seated at the left, play the typical instruments for official dance festivities: namely three shawms and a slide trumpet. The man reaching for a cup of wine plays upon a pipe. The banners of the instruments indicate that they belong to the service of the city of Florence.

Other pictures indicate that it was customary to place "high" instruments on a balcony, while the "low" instruments played close to the dancers. Sometimes the musicians stood among the spectators.

Dance melodies were also sung. In 1465, Giovanni Ambrosio relates that his pupil Ippolita so delighted her father-in-law, Ferrante of Aragon, that "nothing seemed more like paradise to him than to see her dancing and singing." She is said to have danced and sung two new balli, which she composed to tunes which were French songs.

The intermingling of French and Italian cultures became more pronounced after 1494 when the French armies of Charles VIII laid waste to the land. France did not stay long in Italy, but the effects were widespread, and the invaders brought back to France much which they had found in Italy.

Ball of the Duc De Joyeuse, *Clouet,* 1581. *A pavane being danced at a ball given by Catherine de Medici, probably at the time of the* Ballet des Polonais

The Pavane

Pavanes were such slow dances that Arbeau wondered whether they were "too solemn and slow to dance alone with a young girl in the room." This slowness reflects the change in all arts starting in 1498. For, while everything had been speedy and fast in the early 1400s, suddenly, following the Italian campaigns of Charles VIII and Louis XII of France, styles became dignified and dainty. Loudness was decried; simplicity was sought, as reflected in Da Vinci's *Mona Lisa* who wears a very simple hairdo and dress.

It was easy to dance the pavane. The steps were little more than a walk and followed the rhythm with great precision. First the gentleman with a cloak thrown over arm, doffed his hat and gravely bowed before his partner, standing statuesque in her long gown with its train. Then the couple faced forward and commenced the dance, the damsel moving with chaste demeanor and eyes cast down, perhaps glancing at the onlookers with proper modesty.

On the first beat, they glided a step forward with the left foot; on the first beat of the second measure they brought their feet together. In the third and fourth measures they repeated the movement, again placing the left foot forward and again bringing the feet together. Following this, and with one step to each measure, the dancers took a step forward with the right foot, then another step with the left and concluded the figure by bringing both feet together. The performance continued by repeating the entire procedure, or varied it by stepping backward, starting with the right foot rather than the left.

Couples usually preferred to dance forward, for Arbeau warns us that in dancing backward the lady was likely to meet with some hindrance, such as her train, and fall, "an occurrence which would bring censure upon her gentleman and lower him in her graces." Often too, women wore such elaborate trains on the more ceremonious occasions that they had train-bearers, whose motions had to be considered.

A thirty-two-bar tune accompanied the dance, and it was usually repeated. A small drum, called a tabor, usually emphasized the rhythm of the dance, which happens to be similar to that

Air of a pavane (from Arbeau, "La belle qui tiens ma vie")

of the second movement of Beethoven's *Symphony No.* 7. Arbeau writes that the tabor "enabled the feet to come into position according to the required movement."

The music of pavanes was played for many occasions aside from the dance. Arbeau writes: "Our musicians play it when a damsel of good family is taken to the Holy Church to be married, or when musicians head a procession of the chaplains, master and brethren of some guild. . . . These Pavanes are also used in a masquerade when there is a procession of triumphant chariots of gods and goddesses, emperors or kings resplendent in majesty."

The origin of the pavane is veiled in obscurity and no small disagreement was caused by its confusion with the paduane, a late-sixteenth-century dance in 6/8 time. It is debated whether it originated in Italy, or the austere court in Spain. However, most authorities agree that this grave, majestic dance was named after the Italian *pavo* the peacock, since the dancers who followed its slow and stately measures spread their rich garments and fine mantles like that pompous fowl. Furthermore, the Italians customarily used fanciful titles for their dances. But we still cannot learn whether the dance was invented by a dancing master, or just sprang into existence at a noble function.

The pavane developed into a processional pageant of great dignity and imposing display customarily used as the opening dance of all ceremonial balls. Arbeau adds it was used by "kings, princes and great lords, to display themselves on a day of solemn festivity with their fine mantles and robes of ceremony. And these pavanes, played by hautboys and sackbuts, are called the *Grand Bal* and last until those who dance have circled two or three times around, if they do not prefer to dance by advances and retreats." Queen Elizabeth of England was said to have been so fond of the dance that it was more than whispered that in her eyes, excellence in its performance was more valued than statesmanship.

One feature of the pavane was the kiss exchanged by the performers. In the sixteenth century, a trill played by the musical instruments indicated the moment for the salute. This practice was carried over into the dances of nineteenth-century England, where it was related that, during country gatherings, the significant signal was given to the merriment of all present.

Various modifications of the pavane have appeared. Arbeau says that, when it was played a little more rapidly, it was called a *passamezzo.*

The Galliard

The lively *galliard* following a slow and stately pavane formed a natural pair of dances, one fast, the other slow. Often the music of the galliard was a variation of the pavane.

This was the liveliest of lively dances. The very name means gay or jolly in French. It required the nimblest agility and it was said that the performer who had one foot high in the air was "galliard," but if the feet were also crossed, or struck together while in the air, it was *"galliard en perfection."* The characteristic step was the *grue,* wherein one foot was placed somewhat in front of the body while the other was raised as if to kick someone. Our illustration gives some idea of the dance.

The galliard is in 3/4 meter, using the same rhythm as "America"

The galliard (from the "Danceries of Attaignant")

with the accent on the first beat of the measure. On this beat the dancer sprang in to the air and alighted on the sixth beat. Since this left only five steps to the dance, the French called it *cinq-pas* (five steps), which Shakespeare misspelled as "sink-a-piece."

The following steps of the dance follow the music precisely.

1. Spring up, kicking the left foot forward, resting the weight on the right foot.

A Galliard, *woodcut by Jost Amman, 1570. Notice the feet and legs of the dancers.*

2. Spring up, kicking the right foot forward, resting the weight on the left foot.
3. Spring up, kicking the left foot forward, etc.
4. Spring up, kicking the right foot forward, etc.
5. Jump fairly high; if agile, move the legs while in the air.
6. Land! resting the weight on both feet, but with the left foot forward. In the second group of six beats, dancers reverse the footwork, kicking the right foot forward first.

The skill of a dancer was judged by the number of variations of his steps. Sometimes one leg was kicked across the other; sometimes backwards; then again the dancer might merely raise his leg and omit the jump. If eighth notes instead of quarters were used on the first and third beats of each measure, the dancer quickened his steps and necessarily reduced the heights of his springs.

Arena, the dance historian, said that the movements of the dance reminded him of a cockfight. Another writer, Zuccolo, noted in 1549 that the spectators so incited the girl dancers with cries and shouts that they executed lightfooted leaps, lightning-swift turns and kicks, now and then stamping their feet with the greatest abandon.

Queen Elizabeth of England is said to have used its vigorous movements for her morning gymnastics, and at the age of fifty-six, she danced six or seven galliards on arising.

When the galliard first appeared, it included a coquettish pantomime based on the motifs of escape and capture. Arbeau, our authority on sixteenth-century dances, writes:

> When the dancer had chosen a damsel and they had performed the reverance, they took their positions at the end of the room, then made one or two circles around the room, simply walking. Then the dancer released the damsel, whereupon she went dancing to the end of the room, where she continued to dance in the same place. Thereafter, the dancer followed her, came and stood before her and made some passages, turning at will, sometimes to the right, sometimes to the left. This done, she danced up to the other end of the room, where her partner dancing all the time, pursued her to make some other passages before her. And continuing these goings and comings, the dancer made new passages to exhibit his skill until the musicians stopped playing. Then, taking the damsel by the hand, he performed the reverance and thanking her, led her to the place whence he had taken her.

The galliard appeared in Lombardy in the late fifteenth century, being mentioned early in the 1480s. Musical examples appeared early in the sixteenth century. Indeed, the British Museum has a manuscript dating before 1510. The dance lived long after its partner, the pavane, had disappeared from the dance floor. An English court ball featured it in the seventeenth century in the reign of James I. But it has lived on much longer in the purely musical suites played in the music rooms of cultivated society, where we can still hear it today.

6

The Era of Catherine de Medici

The Branle

We now reach the sprightly period of Catherine de Medici (1519-1589), who became queen of France, in 1547.

Until 1500, Italy was the center of arts, and her culture was carried by stagecoach and horseback to other European countries. The full flood was brought to France when Catherine came as bride of the future Henri II. In her wedding party she brought Italian musicians, writers, courtiers, and costumes. These were to play an important part in the development of the ballet.

Catherine goes down in dance history as one of its greatest patrons. From her time, France came to lead the world in the niceties of dancing, and almost every court in Europe had a French dancing master. True, many dances were borrowed from other countries, but these were adapted and refined to the French taste. At first, Catherine sought to break the solemnity of the court by adding lively dances, such as the *galliard,* the *courante,* and *volta,* in which the steps inclined to leaps, hops and runs rather than glides, and we can imagine the great lords and ladies of the court dancing these vigorous and sprightly dances, while dressed in hoop skirts, ruffs and trunk hose. In our picture we note the gentleman carrying his hat and wearing his jeweled sword.

At few periods have so many dances come from the folk, or from so many countries. The French provinces yielded a host of dances. At one famous banquet given in Bayonne in 1565 by Catherine, groups of dancers from almost all the provinces seem to have performed. Girls from Provence danced *voltas* to the accompaniment of cymbals; girls from Brittany performed the *passepied* and *branles gais;* those from Burgundy and Champagne were accompanied by fiddle and shawm, while dancers from Poitou performed to the bagpipe.

The branle became the principal dance after 1550. Today we see similar dancing in our folk dances and square dances. Then, they appeared as rejuvenated forms of the old choral round of the Middle Ages, which had been rejected by the Italian courtiers as undignified and not to be performed by high society unless the performers wore masks. In the round dance, couples danced in closed circles, often holding hands in chainlike succession, performing in the sideward motions typical to the branle. Pantomime also reappeared along with new types of action. In the *branle de Poitou,* the so-called ancestor of the minuet, dancers stamped on the floor like peasants wearing wooden shoes; in the branle des Hermites, they crossed their arms and bowed like hermits. In the Maltese branle, dancers used expressions which Arbeau believed were preserved from a ballet masquerade devised by the knights of Malta, wherein men and girls dressed in Turkish costume danced a round branle with gestures and twisting movements of the body.

The laundresses' branle (*branle des lavandières*) was most interesting; in it dancers clapped hands at intervals to imitate the noise of the bats used by washerwomen on the banks of the Seine, who beat the dirt out of clothes with wooden sticks.

Marguerite de Valois, daughter of Catherine, excelled in the torch branle (*branle de chandelier*), in which a dancer holding a flambeau chose and danced with a partner described by Arbeau as follows:

> Whoever wishes to dance it, takes a candlestick with a lighted candle or torch or brand and dances or walks forward once or twice around the room, looking here and there for the damsel with whom he wishes to dance. When he has chosen the one who pleases him, they dance together for a while, and at last he disposes of her by leaving her at the end of the room and making a reverance, then gives the candlestick into her hands and retires, dancing to his place.
>
> The damsel, holding the candlestick, does as she has seen the young man do, and dances away to choose another man, who eventually takes her place receiving the candlestick from her; in this way all invite each other in turn to dance.

This dance was performed slowly on account of the lighted torch in 2/4 time with the same steps as the *allemande*.

In the branles, dancers moved sidewise rather than forward, and were noted for the balancé, a sort of swaying to and fro. They were performed in a series as in a suite, wherein they progressed from slow to fast. Thus, musicians started the dancing with slower and more sedate forms of the branle double and single for the king and queen, or for older people. After they left the floor, young married couples danced the livelier *branle gai;* next young folk performed rapid branles of Burgundy or Champagne. Another type, the branle of Haut Barrois, named after the old Duchy of Bar, was danced by lackeys and serving wenches, also by youths and girls when masked and disguised as peasants and shepherds. This dance was introduced to the French court in 1556 by Duilly. Capriol suggested it would keep the dancers warm in winter because they continually moved their whole bodies, from feet to shoulders and arms.

In 1636, Father Mersenne, the famous theorist, prescribed a set of five branles of increasing liveliness until all solemnity was dispelled by a *gavotte.*

The Italian version of the branle was named the brando, the English form was called the *brawl.*

In the period of the minuet, after 1664, this popular chain dance gradually lost favor. However, in the eighteenth century, it was reimported from England as the "country dance." In similar fashion it reappears over and over again in America in the folk dances.

The First Ballet de Cour

A favorite entertainment at the court of Catherine de Medici was the *mascarade.* These were elaborate affairs featuring so-called ballets, which were no more than spectacular ballroom dances in which the courtiers took the parts. Following the performance, the audience joined the actors in social dancing.

This was the period which saw the development of all types of dramatic presentation. Thus, while Shakespearean plays were appearing in England, Italy was developing the opera through use of the singing voice, while in France there appeared a type of entertainment with dancing and music spiced with the lilt of dance tunes. In the dramatic episodes of these performances, Catherine encouraged elaborate spectacles.

In 1570, the French Academy of Music and Poetry was founded by the seven Pleiade poets led by de Baïf, who sought to combine movements of the feet and gesticulation to balance the poetic song and instrumental accompaniment.

An offspring of this was the so-called *ballet des polonais,* performed for the Polish ambassadors who came to offer the crown of Poland to Catherine's son, Henri, Duc d'Anjou. Catherine erected a special hall at the Tuileries for this great spectacle, since no permanent theaters existed at the time. Our translation of Brantome's description:

> And all about was an infinite number of torches; she [Catherine] presented the most beautiful ballet that was ever seen on earth . . . which was composed of sixteen ladies and young girls . . . who appeared seated upon the niches of a great silvered rock on wheels. These represented the sixteen provinces of France with the most melodious music ever heard, and, after having made a tour of the room like a parade in camp to let themselves be seen by all, they stepped down from the rock and formed a little battalion of fantastic invention, with viols to the number of thirty sounding pleasantly forth a warlike *air de danse,* and thus they marched in step in perfect time and never getting out of step, stopping a little before their majesties, and danced their ballet, most fantastically conceived, and with so many turns, counterturns and detours, interlacings and blendings, such advances and arrests, in which not one lady ever failed to turn in her place nor in her rank, that all present were surprised how much in such a maze order never became disorder . . . and this fantastic ballet continued at least an hour, and being concluded, all these ladies were presented to the King, to the Queen, to the King of Poland, to Monsieur, his brother, to the King and Queen of Navarre and the other lords of France and Poland. . . .

This ballet marked a fashion for figure dancing which apparently had not been seen in France since it so greatly impressed the observers.

The greatest dance performance of the era was the so-called first *ballet de cour,* performed in 1581 for the marriage of the Duc de Joyeuse and the queen's sister, Mlle de Vaudemont. This great spectacle was produced at the cost of three million six hundred thousand francs.

Hundreds of people packed the assembly, sitting along the walls of the room as was customary. Our illustration shows the royal

Ballet Comique de la Royne, *Balthasar de Beaujoyeux, Paris,* 1582. Courtesy the New York Metropolitan Museum of Art, Harris Brisbane Dick Fund, 1930

family sitting at one end under a canopy. To the king's right is the arbor of Pan, with a grotto flanked by illuminated trees. To his left, framed by clouds, is a golden vault, where bands of musicians performed upon many varied instruments. These echoed the voices of the singers and played introductions and interludes. At the extreme end of the hall is the garden and castle of Circe, the enchantress, flanked by the entrances for the dancers or the cars bearing personages.

The performance commenced at about ten in the evening with an overture. Suddenly a gentleman came fleeing from Circe's palace. Terrified and wiping his forehead, he addressed verses to the king, begging his succor from Circe. Hardly had he finished when Circe appeared and sang her "Complaint at Having Lost a Gentleman." Next, a procession of sirens and tritons with tails made of scales of gold and burnished silver entered singing together in the first *Intermède.*

The singers in the golden vault answered them, announcing the arrival of a floatlike fountain, bearing La Princess de Lorraine, les Duchesses de Mersoeur, de Guise, de Nevers, etc.; etc., representing Thetis and Glaucis in the midst of the Nereids. At the base of the elaborate jet were the chief dancers of the evening, the Naiads, arranged in plastic groups. Following them came the chariot and choir of eight tritons.

After the parade had halted and an exchange of verse had taken place between Glaucis and Thetis, the *corps de ballet* of Naiads descended and began the *première entrée de ballet.*

Thus began this great dance spectacle which continued in ever-increasing grandeur for over five hours. But the evening had not concluded until social dances were performed, and the courtiers in court dress had danced with the performers in costume.

This ballet was the first modern integrated theatrical dance drama. It unified the elements of tournament, masquerade, and pastorale. It was based upon a text and used completely composed music. The dances were founded upon the dances of the day but were more loosely constructed. Thus, one of the most charming tunes we still know today as "Amaryllis." It is composed in the style of a gavotte, which was one of the favored social dances of the time.

Air de Clochette (from Ballet Comique de la Reine, *and often called "Amaryllis")*

The Bourrée

Among the sixteenth-century dances included in baroque suites we find the *bourrée.* It is mentioned at the famous festival at Bayonne in 1565 as a folk dance performed before Catherine de Medici by natives of Bourgogne in homage to the province.

The bourrée is described as most vigorous and earthy, originally being a sort of clog dance executed with precise energy by the peasants. It was frequently danced and sung by the winemakers as they crushed the grapes in vats by stamping and dancing on them with their bare feet.

When danced by groups, a line of men and a line of women faced each other, and, as the files danced back and forth, the leader on the right and the dancer opposite left their lines and exchanged places. One after the other, all their neighbors followed suit.

When performed by couples, the bourrée was danced open style without touching hands, to the accompaniment of the bagpipes and hurdy-gurdy. The women gracefully held their skirts and the men danced with arms raised high. This was a mimetic dance in which the woman hovered round the man as if to approach him. He retreated and returned to flee again. Finally, snapping his fingers, he stamped his feet, uttered a vigorous cry as if to express his strength and masculinity, whereupon the woman yielded.

This folk dance of the Auvergne was once regarded as no less than scandalous. It is related that when Francis I was on his way to fetch Catherine de Medici for her marriage to his son, the dauphin, Henry II, he stopped with his suite at Clermont-Ferrand in Auvergne, where he was given a splendid reception followed by sumptuous entertainments in which many bourrées were performed, and undoubtedly their indecent and degenerate offshoot, the *goignade,* mentioned by Flechier.

> The ecclesiastical personages in the suite of Francis I were scandalized by the performance of this dance—they resolved to have

> it forbidden by the Pope. The question was submitted to the Sacred College. The College was disposed to place an interdict on the dance when one of the judges, probably Cardinal Duprat, wisely observed that one could not very well condemn the dance without seeing it. Therefore, they called into the Consistory Hall a group of young men and women from Auvergne who belonged in the party of the Cardinal Minister (Duprat) and these young people interpreted a few figures of the real bourrée. On seeing this, the foreheads of the judges lost their wrinkles, their eyes shone and their severity was changed to admiration. The members of the Sacred College began to beat the time with their feet and their hands in approval. Then they in turn took part in the dancing. Soon the Consistory Hall was turned into a grand ballroom; even the cardinals danced the bourrée, which was of course absolved unanimously by the judges.

All the heavy, simple, and crude peasant characteristics disappeared from the dance after it was introduced to the French court, although it retained the figures in which the women moved coquettishly about the men as they advanced and returned. In court the bourrée was a skipping dance, performed best when skirts were short.

The fastidious and ceremonious courts of later years never fully accepted the bourrée, and it was retained chiefly as a theatrical specialty for the ballet and as a local folk dance.

Bourée (from Bach's "Overture in F")

In the ballet, its step pattern is somewhat like the gavotte, being written with four beats to a measure and followed by a second composition in the same form. But the bourrée starts on the fourth beat and the second beat can be accented. Furthermore, it has a smoother, more gliding style.

The Gavotte

The gavotte was a new dance in the time of Catherine de Medici, and its steps are listed as a mixture of branles and galliard movements. It then seemed to possess aspects of a wooing or wedding pantomime. Arbeau wrote:

> When those taking part have danced a little, one couple detach themselves from the rest and execute a few passages in the center of of the room in view of the others. Then, the first dancer proceeds to kiss all the damsels in the room and his partner kisses all of the young men, after which they return to their rightful places. This accomplished, the second couple do likewise and so on through the entire group. Some confer the prerogative of kissing upon the host and his partner alone, and at the conclusion the said damsel, who carries a garland or bouquet, presents it to the dancer who must next be host and pay the musicians. . . .

According to Arbeau's directions, the dancers first took three steps forward—right foot, left and right—then they brought the left foot up to the right. This required four beats. Next, they repeated the procedure, beginning with the left foot instead of the right. Try this in gavotte rhythm. To vary the steps, dancers freely added galliard steps.

The rhythm of the gavotte gives a distinctive sprightliness that captures the spirit of the ancient rustic dance which originated in the Alpine province of Gapençais. Here, the peasants, called *Gavots,* gaily trod its measures, now lifting their feet high off the ground, now stamping their wooden shoes.

Originally the music was in 2/2 time, but, as the performance continued, they added quicker and more elaborate steps, until it became a moderately rapid 4/4.

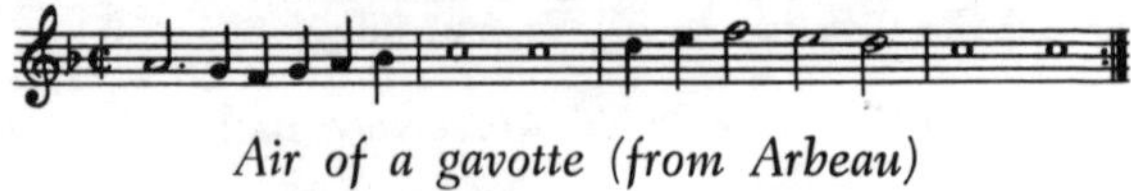

Air of a gavotte (from Arbeau)

Between 1600 and 1700, the gavotte was introduced in Paris. In its new surroundings it assumed many new aspects, losing much of its refreshing *joie de vivre,* and absorbing much of the formality and dignity of the court. In 1636, Father Mersenne described it as follows:

> One or two rounds: then the first leader of the branle à mener bows before his lady, dances light steps in front of her, bows again and returns to his place with her, all couples repeat this in succession; then there is general bowing and the ladies are led back to their seats.

Amid all this bowing, it seems as if the Gavots would not recognize their dance.

Gavottes are frequently followed by another gavotte called a *musette*. This movement, which has a more rural flavor, is followed by a repetition of the first gavotte, and the sequence—gavotte, musette, gavotte—is an example of the survival of the old form of contrasting pairs of dances, one of which was a step dance and the other a hop dance.

The musette derives its name from the pedal bass of the old French bagpipe called a *musette* or *corne de musse,* which has a drone bass tone accompanying every tune played upon it.

As we have said, one of the most charming tunes for a gavotte is known as "Amaryllis," dating from Catherine's famous ballet of 1581.

The Carrousel

When the old medieval tournaments, with their knightly combat on horseback or afoot, went out of style after Henry II of France was killed in a joust, his queen, Catherine de Medici, decided to eliminate the bloodshed and develop the carrousel, a tournament in which knights and cavalrymen divided into troops and executed various maneuvers and often performed scenic shows and allegorical dances. Today the carrousel has come to mean a merry-go-round with wooden horses executing a sort of puppet revolution similar to the grand maneuvers of the sixteenth century.

One of the first horseback ballets was given on June 25, 1565, in Bayonne, where Catherine and her sons met Isabelle of France, who had become queen of Spain. The participants were divided into two groups of eight cavaliers; one group was supposed to be British and the other Irish—even then two warring peoples. The leaders were the king, Charles IX, and his brother, later to become Henry III. After a parade with chariots bearing personages dressed as Virtues, Muses, Amors, and Venus, the fighting groups appeared and staged a parade and action in which first one fought against one, then two against two. Next, the riders formed a large cross, keeping equidistant from one another, and performed different figure movements by approaching each other, changing places, etc. Finally they appeared to fight in a crowd, changing places and

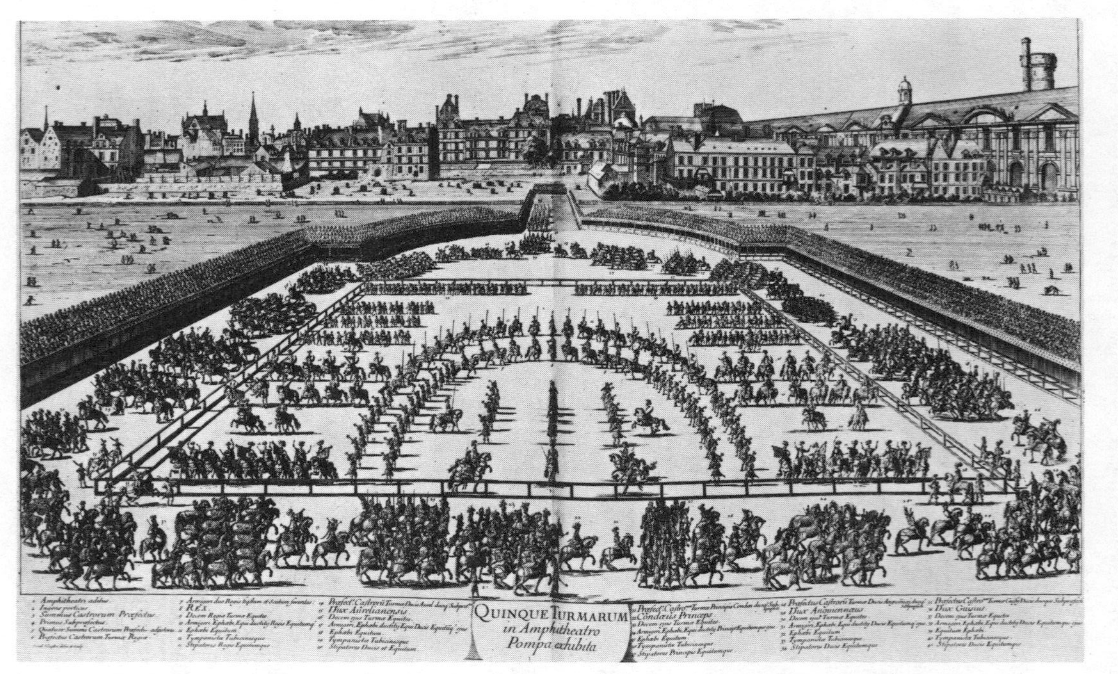

Quinque Turmarum in Amphiteatro Pompa Exhibita, *Israel Sylvestre, from Chalcographie du Louvre*. Courtesy the New York Metropolitan Museum of Art, Harris Brisbane Dick Fund, 1930

intermixing pell-mell until separated by a great display of fireballs. We can assume that music accompanied much of the action. The tournaments of old had their ceremonial trumpet fanfares and instrumental backgrounds, as well as the singing and strumming of ballads and love songs to the ladies.

In time the equestrian ballet developed into a highly elaborate entertainment for the courts, with special musical backgrounds. One of the greatest was performed at immense cost in 1666, in Vienna, for the emperor, Leopold I. Known as *The Contest between Air and Water,* it was performed in the yard of the castle with such properties as an immense vessel, a cloud car, and similar machines—all built for the performance. After a ballet depicting the elements battling gods favoring the water or the air, the machines were pushed aside for the equestrians. The vocal music was written by an Italian composer Bertali, while Schmelzer composed the music for the equestrians. Two high trumpets, the *clarini,* played the melodies. According to the custom for outdoor festivals, the *clarini* were probably separated from the rest of the orchestra, which may have consisted of four or five stringed instruments and many brasses and woodwinds. The dance music still in existence includes a courante (an entry played by trumpets and tympani upon the arrival of his majesty and courtiers), a jig for the entrance of the knights on foot ,the customary *folia,* which from the time of Catherine was used for the entrance and maneuvers of the equestrians and a very slow allemande for the solemn movements of the emperor on his white Lipizzaner horse, and finally, a sarabande for leavetaking at the conclusion of the ballet.

The equestrian ballet lives today in the wonderful shows of the famous Lipizzaner horses. In 1580, the ancestors of these beautiful, snow-white Arabian horses were sent to Austria from Spain as a gift to the emperor. Noted for their intelligence and their capability for performing intricate and difficult movements, they soon became the favored horse for exhibitions and were specially trained in the imperial stables in Lipizzani. With the fall of the monarchy early in the twentieth century, the stables lost their sponsor; but in 1931 they were regenerated. Today the ballet of the Lipizzaners is one of the prides of Vienna and this wonderful exhibition of superb horsemanship travels around the world.

7

German Dancing

WHILE THE ELEGANT ARISTOCRATS of France and Italy were performing pavanes and galliards, Germans were dancing quite differently, for Germany lay outside the more cultured countries where the dancing masters trained the youth in courtly graces. As late as 1598, Prince Ludwig of Anhalt-Kothen was surprised that the Florentines did not dance "with jugglers hands nor did they roll their shoulders now here, now there." In general, German life was on a lower level, and the people preferred their native dances which had remained virtually unchanged from the Middle Ages.

However, like most of Europe, the Germans had a slow introductory dance followed by a lively after-dance often termed TANZ. The slow introductory dance for open couples seems to be that transported to France and called the *allemande* (German). Arbeau writes:

> The allemande is a plain dance of certain gravity, familiar to the Germans and, I believe, is one of our most ancient dances, for we are descended from the Germans. You can dance it in company, because when you have joined hands with a damsel, several others may fall into line behind you, each with his partner. And you will all dance together in duple time, moving forwards, or if you wish backwards, three steps and a grêve (a hop on one foot and a kick with the other), or merely move and point the foot to the right or left. . . . When you have reached the end of the hall you can dance while turning around without letting go of your damsel, and the dancers who follow you will do the same. When the musicians finish this first part, each dancer stops and engages in light conversation with his damsel and then you will begin over again for the second part. When you come to the third part, you will dance it to a quicker, more lively duple time with the same steps but introducing little springs as in the coranto.

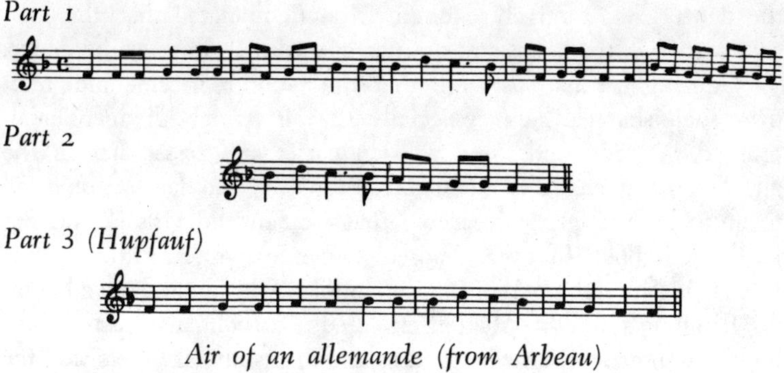

Air of an allemande (from Arbeau)

This third section is apparently the lively hop dance (*Hupfauf*). The historian Praetorius, in the early seventeenth century writes that the dance usually had three repetitions each of which had four bars. Each of the three dances was usually a variation, and the musicians improvised in each in the repetitions.

Although we read of allemandes for four centuries, we must realize that the term refers to several types of dance and music. The old dance described above and composed in even time disappeared in the seventeenth century. The court of Louis XIV adopted another version at the time of the annexation of Alsace. Bach had a slow and somewhat songlike contrapuntal movement, and, at the court of Napoleon, there was a third type, which was that of Beethoven and von Weber.

Besides these respectable open couple dances, Germans indulged in dances of such exuberance that they were rough indeed. We read that couples screamed, shouted, and snatched each other; men tossed their partners high into the air in what seems to be closed couple dances such as the later *landler* and *waltz*.

The German engraver Aldegrever depicts many of the features of German dancing. The lady usually dances to the right of her partner, although the performers may dance back to back, possibly while changing sides in passing. Cheek-to-cheek dancing was in high favor, and, when Montaigne visited the Fuggers in Augsburg in 1480, he wrote in his diary that the man held both hands on the back of his partner and clasped in such close embrace that their faces touched. In German and also English dancing, the kiss was a part of the dance. Yet, strangely enough, Montaigne noted that the men sat apart from the ladies and did not mix with them after the dance.

Dancing became so rough that the Church became indignant over such shamelessness, especially that in which the gentleman grasped the lady under her wooden corset and tossed her in the air. Town councils ruled upon the costumes of the dancers, objected to mutual claspings, and ordered that women and girls should not be thrown about. In 1550, Andreas Oseander wrote to Hieronymus Besola in Nuremburg that all the couples who danced together at his daughter's wedding had been fined. Bartholmaus Sastrow was highly indignant when penalized by the magistrate at Griefswald for similar conduct at his own wedding.

8

The Merry Dances of Queen Elizabeth

QUEEN ELIZABETH I delighted in all the gay dances introduced in France by her contemporary, Catherine de Medici. Elizabeth, herself, was a very lively person and not always as regal as her state portraits might indicate. She often expressed herself with tremendous oaths and coarse actions. When Leicester knelt to receive his earldom, she tickled the back of his neck with a feather. She even spat at a courtier whose coat offended her taste.

Elizabeth had an insatiable love of pleasure and spectacle. She was particularly fond of the livelier dances. It is known that she delighted in the high jumps and hops cultivated by the English. Once she gained the compliments of Melville, the Scottish ambassador, who remarked that the queen of England could hop much higher than Her Majesty, Mary, Queen of Scots. Although Melville may have seen her dancing an English country dance or a galliard, in all probability, she was hopping in a *volta,* the precursor of the waltz, which Sir John Davies beautifully describes in his poem, "Orchestra."

> Yet is there one the most delightful kind,
> A lofty jumping or a leaping round:
> When arm in arm two dancers are entwined
> And whirl themselves with strict embracements bound
> And still their feet an anapest do sound!
>   An anapest is all their music's song
>   Whose first two feet are short, and third is long!

Air of a volta (from Arbeau)

Bal a la cour des Valois, *anonymous. The work is similar to the English painting* La Volta at the English Court, *revealing Queen Elizabeth dancing with the Earl of Leicester.* Courtesy Rennes, Musée des Beaux Arts

Our picture, *Bal à la Cour des Valois,* bears an astounding likeness to an English picture entitled *La Volta,* in which we see Elizabeth dancing a volta, with the Earl of Leicester grasping the queen under her wooden corset in order to lift her in the air, all to the accompaniment of a string band.

In Elizabeth's day, dancing was the usual entertainment after banquets. On such occasions, the men usually unhasped their swords and gave them to the pages or torch-bearers while the hall was cleared by laying the table tops and trestles against the wall. At the end of the entertainment, prizes were frequently given to the best woman dancer.

Dancing was the pastime for all classes, from the highest to the lowest. The merry month of May was ushered in with all types of gay dances, from that about the maypole to the performances of morris dancers with hobbyhorses and dragons.

In England, the branle was known as the "brawls." This dance was not a solemn branle double. Indeed the word brawls as used today indicates the boisterous nature of the dance. Sir Christopher Hatton often led a rustic version of the dance, which was evidently particularly enjoyed at the rowdy conclusion of rustic weddings.

Good fellows must go learne to daunce
    The brydale is full near a:
There is a brall come out of France
    The first ye harde this year a,
But I must leape and thous must hoppe
    And we must turn all three a:
The fourth must bounce it like a toppe,
    And so we shall agree a.

Elizabeth danced until her last years. It is recorded that in 1600, when she was sixty-eight, she honored the wedding of Lord Herbert at Black Friars, where she was entertained by a masque performed by eight richly attired ladies, who, "'after they had donne all their own ceremonies, chose from the audience more ladies to dawnce the measures. The leader, Mrs. Fetton, approached the queen and woed her to dawnce, and Her Majesty, after exchanging a few pithy remarks, rose and dawnced."

The English Masque

In England under the Tudor kings (1485-1603), as in Europe, elaborate entertainments and revelry followed the decline of tournaments and jousts.

Anciently, a motley group of disguised and masked persons amused the guests at a party or fete by the unexpectedness of their arrival and chance actions. This developed a certain dramatic quality when the disguised persons performed prepared dances and speeches. In time the procedures became more elaborate, and the costumed group arrived in a chariot or pageant machine, then danced a stately basse dance or a livelier *ronde* and other fashionable aristocratic dances. Thus, at the wedding of Prince Arthur to Catherine of Aragon in 1501, there was the following grand pageant:

> On Thursday evening the Court again assembled in Westminster Hall, and as soon as silence had been secured two marvelous pageants were disclosed at the lower end of the chamber. These pageants, which were fastened together with a golden chain, represented two great mountains, one of them green, full of all kinds of trees and herbs and flowers, the other like a dark rock scorched with the sun and full of metals and precious stones. On the sides of the first hill sat twelve disguised noblemen with musical instruments and on the second hill sat ladies also with "claricordes," dulcimers, etc. among them a lady dressed like the Princess of Spain, seated upon the topmost peak. As the pageant moved up the Hall to the king, "both companies of disguisers played so sweetly and with such noyse that in my mynde it was the first such pleasant myrth and property that was ever herde in England of longe season."

As soon as the pageants came to a standstill the lords danced "deliberate, and pleasantly," and then "the ladies descended and coupled with the lords and daunced there a long season many and divers rondes and newe daunces full curiously and with most wonderfull counteynance. In the meane season the two mountaines departed and evanished out of presence and sight."

When pleasure-loving Henry VIII became king in 1509, the revelry assumed added dimensions. Pageants and disguisings took on the aspects of the later masques; sometimes they were combined with mummeries, which were a sort of play. In 1512, Henry introduced the notorious Italian masquerie to his rather scandalized court. In these the masked performers danced with the spectators. This shocked the ladies of the English court, since they had no knowledge of the identity of the masked persons who approached them for the dance, for the masquers were entirely concealed by full Italian robes wrought in gold and golden visors, with masques and caps to hide their heads. Accordingly some ladies left the room and this form of entertainment was not very successful. However, it did influence the development of the Elizabethan masque, wherein the masqueraders danced with the audience.

When the English court masque finally developed, it was not necessarily literature but dance and dance music. Shakespeare describes such a masque in *Romeo and Juliet* as well as in his *Henry VIII*. In masques, where the music began with an invocation, then masquers, representing celestial or mythological beings, descended to dance their entry. Following various set dances, the program led to the revels, when the noble masked dancers were urged to choose and dance with a courtly spectator of the opposite sex. Then ensued an hour-long performance of the dances of the day, until the masquers were called off, and after a last departing dance returned to their original hideout in a glade or cloud.

It is to be noted that the performers were not trained professional dancers, but courtiers, usually of noble birth, who performed the dances of the day. The music of the masque was the introduction and dance accompaniment as well as vocal setting, not unlike those in the French court ballet which was reaching a high state of development at the same time under Catherine de Medici. The music for the ballroom dances of the English revels was that of the *measure*—a sort of organized procession—the galliards, corantos, and other popular dance forms.

The Jig

The jig was an English dance that became a great favorite of European composers for two centuries. There are at least thirteen spellings of the name, from *gigue, gique, gig,* to *jigge* and *jig.*

It was once believed that the name came from the old word for the fiddle, *giga* or *geige,* which might have been the instrument accompanying the dance. However, the early English jig was mostly accompanied by the tabor and pipe. And it is most likely that the word came from Iceland's *geiga,* which refers to something round or revolving. . . . Thus we have the whirligig, a carriage called a gig; Shakespeare wrote, "go whip thy gig," meaning "whip thy top." Furthermore, dancers of a jig spun around, and most jig music possesses whirling characteristics, given by rapid triplet figures.

The jig was first mentioned in 1559 by Sir Henry Sidney, who, in a letter to Queen Elizabeth, enthused over the dancing of Irish jigs by the Anglo-Saxon ladies of Galway who were "very beautiful, magnificently dressed and first class dancers."

By 1581, the dance was most popular in England. Shakespeare noted, in *Love's Labor Lost,* "But to jig off a tune at the tongue's end, canary to it with your feet." Jigs were frequently included in plays, revels and masques, being particularly favored by the student lawyers studying at the inns of the court, who enlivened their scholarly activities by dancing. At this time a jig also meant a short comic sketch performed during the intermission of, or after, a play. Shakespeare called them the leading spirit of the theatrical repertoire, where two or three performers appear to have sung and danced some very lively, even grotesque figures, which may have included such acrobatic feats as leaping and vaulting.

As a social dance, the jig was very gay, requiring rapid, intricate footwork and lively stamping of heels. It was properly intended for solo performance, and reached its greatest popularity in the early seventeenth century, when it was danced by courtier and country folk alike. But, by the middle of the century, it became regarded as a purely instrumental form.

There was a great difference among the jigs of England, Ireland, and Scotland. The Irish jig seems to reflect the sentimental and adventurous traits of the land, being a sort of symbolic picture of Irish life, in which the first figures depicted lovemaking, wedding, and marriage, followed by the troubles of married life, repentance, and, in the concluding section, age and death.

Jigs were introduced to Continental Europe after the middle of the seventeenth century, being presented by troupes of English actors and musicians in Germany, France and Italy. In 1685, Lully introduced a gigue into his operas in France. Other composers followed, but in operatic productions the dance was greatly changed. Even in England the dance was altered, and eventually the word came to mean little more than a light rhythmic figure.

Originally the gigue was in 3/8 meter, but since writers of ancient music did not divide their tunes with barlines as we do today, the length of the measure was stretched to 6/8 and even 12/8. Italian composers preferred 12/8. Indeed, some, like Corelli, began the practice of concluding their sonatas with an allegro movement in 12/8, thus making them a sort of an Italian gigue. This custom became accepted in the suites of baroque composers, where it became their practice to bring suites to a brilliant conclusion with a gay and vivacious gigue. In this manner the lively dance eventually became known as an instrumental form.

The Hornpipe

The hornpipe was a well-known dance in Elizabethan England, but its roots lay far back in antiquity. Chaucer (1340-1400) mentions it in reference to a rude type of instrument—"The Hornpipes of Cornwailes"—and evidently this instrument was made from the horn of an ox or other animal.

The bagpipe seems to be a typical instrument for the dance in earlier times. Indeed there is a famous English composition for the virginal "Hornepype" by Hugh Aston (1509-1547). This amazingly long work for the period is based on a drone bass typical of music composed for the bagpipe family.

Little is known about the dance steps of earlier hornpipes, but, near the year 1800, a Scottish dancing master wrote the following instructions for performing some steps of the dance:

"Slips and shuffle forwards, spleet and floorish backwards. Hyland steps forwards, twist around backwards, cross stocks aside and swing forwards, and finally hop forwards and backwards, etc."

More recently, the hornpipe became associated with the British sailors who were actually required to learn the dance, possibly because it required no partners and could be danced on the small decks of the old sailing ships.

Capt. John Cook, the famous navigator, asserted that the dance was useful in keeping his sailors in good health during their voyage around the world. For, when calm weather lessened the necessity of work, he made them dance, usually a hornpipe, to the sound of a fiddle.

Admiral Nelson, victor of the famous Battle of Trafalgar, recommended the following accomplishment to a young naval officer, "You will see almost the necessity of it when employed in foreign countries; indeed the honour of the nation is so often entrusted to sea-officers that there is no accomplishment that will not shine with peculiar luster in them."

As a result of its association with the sea, the dance figures were so altered that nearly every one seemed symbolical of nautical activity. First, the arms of the sailor were folded while the upper part of his body remained in a state of repose, as if in calm defiance of the elements. Meanwhile the lower limbs moved vigorously. Sometimes the body sank and rose as feet were crossed, first on one side, then on the other, as if the sailor were riding the waves with his ship. Soon the arms became vigorously active; the dancer hitched up his trousers and careened about the room. He pantomimed hauling in the ropes either by vigorously pulling hand over hand or by energetically pulling from side to side. Now he hauled in the windlass; then he seemed to row off to shore; all the while his feet executed rough and rollicking steps typical of a seaman.

This activity could be performed without music if necessary, or with the inevitable bagpipe or fiddle found on most naval vessels at the time. On the other hand there was a special wooden pipe with holes and fitted with a reed mouthpiece, which was found on ships.

Handel and composers of his time included a hornpipe in their suites. Note the hornpipe in Handel's "Fireworks Music."

The *furry dance* is a lively old street dance of Helston, Cornwall, performed at the advent of spring and anciently accompanied by the galoubet and tambourine, i.e., a pipe and drum, colloquially called "whittle and dub." It is a processional-type line dance like the polonaise and farandole.

The *farandole* is a lively dance in 6/4 meter, native to Provence and the Basques of Bayonne. Curt Sachs calls it a classic example of the arch dance, wherein couples pass under arched hands as in "London Bridge." It is described in Daudet's novel *Numa Romestan* and used in his play *Arlesienne,* for which Bizet composed a suite. Gounod also included a farandole in his opera *Mireille.*

9

The Influence of Spanish Bass Patterns

THE BAROQUE PERIOD began in Italy with violent attacks on the old contrapuntal style by the so-called Florentine *Camerata,* who created the opera in their efforts to recreate Greek drama. The new form was based on the principle of a solo voice with accompaniment, a fact which sped the chordal approach to music by using a melody supported by chords and harmonies formed upon a bass pattern called the *basso continuo* or thorough bass.

In the new style, the basso continuo was either freely invented or followed certain bass patterns derived from dance melodies. The most common were the *passamezzo antico* and the *passamezzo moderno,* the *romanesca,* the *ruggiero,* the *folia* and later the *chaconne* and the *passacaglia.* These spread throughout Europe. In England they became the basis of the music of the court masque and improvised ballads. The forms have persisted for centuries and even appear in the popular music of the twentieth century in certain types of the blues, boogie, and later styles.

In the baroque they soon became classified in stylized dance music as sets of variations fittingly called a *partita* in Italy, a *partie* in France, and so forth. Another term for this was "divisions," which indicated splitting the notes of a melody into shorter notes for a variation.

The lute played an important part in creating the new style of music. It is an instrument resembling a small pear-shaped mandolin with a fretted fingerboard. Lutes were usually plucked, although the chitarrone variety corresponded to our modern bowed double-bass viol.

Although lutes could play contrapuntal music, newer composers soon perceived that their most natural style employed twanging chords, strummed at an easy distance apart. Hence the instrument was better suited for accompaniments where it supplied chords. However in the early operas, groups of lutes of various sizes were used in the orchestration.

The association of the bass melodies with Spanish musicians deserves special attention. Spain had reached the zenith of her power by the mid-sixteenth century. The Moorish influence still remained and South American gold had brought power. Spain ruled the Netherlands, and, through a series of marriages, she was united to the English as well as the Hapsburgs of Austria, who were the Holy Roman emperors of Europe. This encouraged a great Hispaniolization in art and fashion. Europeans adopted a Spanish costume. Men wore tight-fitting trunk hose, padded sleeves, the cloak, and the stiff Spanish ruff.

In music, Spanish influence stemmed from Spain's extensive folklore in poetry and music as well as the Spanish interest in improvising variations—all carried over from the Arabian fondness for songs accompanied by plucked stringed instruments. The lute itself came from the Orient and derived its name from the Arabic *'al'ud,* while the Oriental habit of varying the accompaniment to a song of many verses and of making this accompaniment more and more interesting and more and more florid contributed greatly to the development of the variation form.

The Spanish lute writers began to lay the foundations of chordal music as early as 1535 (Luis Milan). Then in 1553, Diego Ortiz seems to have published the first examples of the extended bass melodies.

The appearance of the guitar and its introduction to Italy swept Europe into chordal music, which was abetted by a group of Spanish guitar virtuosi who achieved tremendous popularity. In turn, this created a wave of amateur guitar study. In 1606, Montesardo introduced a simplified guitar notation indicating a set of about a dozen chords by single letters, which quickly enabled the dilletanti to strum a continuo on the latest dance hit after a few easy lessons. Thus the tradition of polyphonic playing was soon replaced by the thumb-sweeping *rasguedo* style of strumming arpeggiated chords, often using the ground bass tunes.

Of these, the *romanesca* was not a dance, but was the name of a certain galliard melody fashionable in the sixteenth century. Arbeau noted, "We always played on our lutes and guitars the galliard called 'la Romanesque'; but I held it trite and trivial."

Romanesca bass (from Alonso de Mudarra's romanesca "O Guardame las Vacas")

The romanesca tune was not Spanish but Italian. Indeed, the word signifies a Roman tune. However it became associated with the Spanish tune "O Guardam las Vacas," which was the first line of a text, and it was included in the Spanish lute books of Narvaez in 1538. Baroque composers used it widely for their variations, and it was also used in the *passamezzo.*

The passamezzo (or *passemezzo* or *passo e mezzo*) was an extremely important Italian dance, which became known in Elizabethan England as the *measures,* a word derived from the anglicized pronunciation "passing measures." In Italy the passamezzo seems to have taken the place of the pavane, for, with the appearance of a passamezzo in Antonio Rotta's *Intablatura del Lauto* (1546), the pavane seems to have disappeared in Italy, although it lived on much longer in France and England. After 1636, it was no longer performed.

The term "passo e mezzo" means a pace and a half, which might seem to refer to dance steps. However, it can also refer to dance music in halved-note values, since mezzo can refer to the diminution (halving) of note values as indicated in the alla-breve sign. In apparent confirmation, Arbeau wrote, "When musicians played the pavane more rapidly it was called a passamezzo."

The music of passamezzo dances was not original, but was a variation of the Romanesca "Guardam las Vacas." Pieces composed on this bass were termed "passamezzo antico." The passamezzo moderno (or nuovo) is written in major and has tonic and dominant harmonies in quicker tempo.

The passamezzo bass was long a favorite with composers, and its use spread far afield from the dance. Often the passamezzo

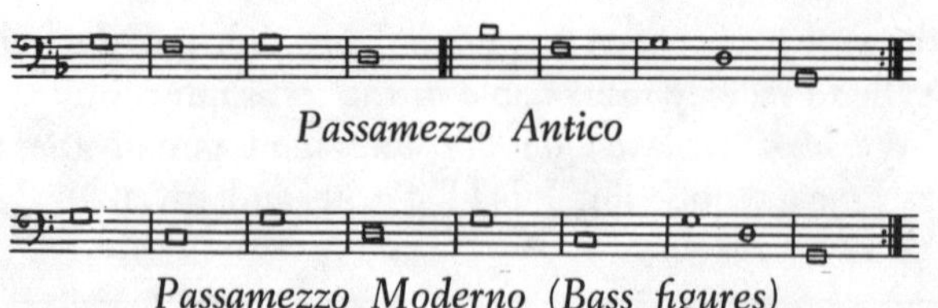

Passamezzo Antico

Passamezzo Moderno (Bass figures)

was coupled with the saltarello; sometimes there is a passamezzo pavane with the saltarello. Examples may be found in the famous Fitzwilliam virginal book.

The *ruggiero* was a similar basso ostinato tune. The musicologist Alfred Einstein shows that it was used for the recitation of the great epic poems of the Renaissance, adding that the name refers to a stanza "Ruggier Qual sempre fui . . ." from Ariostos's "Orlando furioso" which is illustrated below. The earliest extant ruggiero composition is that of Diego Ortiz (1553).

Ruggiero (bass)

Ruggiero (theme from Aristo's "Orlano Furioso")

The *folia* has one of the most curious stories in music history. The name is derived from a dance customarily associated with the Portuguese carnival. Curt Sachs says it was a fertility dance connected with the ancient Portuguese vegetation charm, and, like the morris dance, had men dancing and singing as women. In 1611, Covarrubbias described it in *Tesoro de la Longua Castellana* as a noisy dance with many step patterns accompanied by castanets and other instruments. In it, some dancers carried masked figures on their shoulders while other men, dressed as girls with pointed sleeves, danced, turned, and played the castanets. So loud was the din and so furiously did the dancers fling themselves, that it seemed as if they had gone crazy, as the name *folía* (lunacy) suggests.

The folia is associated with a confusing series of dances involving various periods and countries. The Spaniards adopted the folia as a sort of wooing dance performed by one or two persons with many erotic gestures to a tune with a sarabandelike melody in 3/4 time. However, this sixteenth- and seventeenth-century dance seems more like a galliard than the wild Portuguese folía.

Folia bass

Folia (variation from Corelli's "Twelfth Sonata for Violin with figured bass")

In Italy, the Portuguese dance became associated with a specific tune dating back to an Italian model called "La Gamba" or "La Cara Cosa," which was the nickname for a *famosa ballerina* who danced before Isabella d'Este in 1535. In England the tune was used for an ostinato bass in one of the oldest lute manuscripts, "Blame Not My Lute." Later, the folia became associated with the entrance and maneuvers of equestrians in the equestrian ballets.

Otto Gombosi, the musicologist, in an article in 1940 attempted to explain how the dance became associated with lunacy, the jester and fool of the moresca, as well as the horseback ballet and the courtly Italian dance. He connected it to the specific equestrian ballet performed before Catherine de Medici in 1565, in which the writer Ivanoff states that the mock combatants "fought in a crowd (*combatterent en foulle*) changing places and intermingling pell-mell . . ." From this, the German chronicler of tournaments, Reuxner, called this section of the ballet the "Follia." Gombosi also connects the folia or the fool or jester to a phase of the morris dance in which a stylized sham battle is fought between masked dancers in which the fool appeared as well as hobbyhorses. Gombosi is of the opinion that the fool was the medium through whom the sham battle became associated with the courtly basso ostinato by means of his connection with all court entertainments, including those with courtly tunes performed on courtly instruments.

North of the Pyrenees, the basso ostinato of the folia became more popular than the dance, and is known as Les Folies d'Espagne. Concert audiences know it best from Corelli's variations in his Twelfth Violin Sonata with figured bass, although other composers have used the melody.

Two other important ground basses appeared in about 1600: the chaconne (in Italian, *ciacona*) and the passacaglia (in French, *passacaille*).

The *chaconne* derived its name from the Spanish *chacona* (pretty), and was a dance for a solo performer. Cervantes asserts it was a Negro primitive dance imported to the court of Phillip II and then modified by Castilian gravity. It was first mentioned in connection with Central America, the origin of so many dances. In 1599 Simon Agudo. wrote several verses for the entremés of Platillo, given at the wedding of Phillip III in which he extended an invitation to visit Tampico in Mexico and dance the Chaconna.

The dance was once regarded as more unbridled and sensual than the early sarabande, but after its introduction to France, it was transformed into a social dance, customarily performed at the conclusion of balls. It became a great favorite on the stage and Compan described its changing steps in the French ballet. In the nineteenth century, a four-beat step with large and high movements was known as the *pas de chaconne*. Lully adopted the custom of concluding his operas with a chaconne and established the precedent. Gluck in the eighteenth century used the form in his opera *Orfeo* and his ballet *Iphigenie en Aulide*. Handel used the form, and Bach wrote two of the most remarkable musical examples, one being that of his "Fourth Violin Sonata," the other, the "Goldberg Variations," which are founded on a chaconne bass with a sarabande rhythm.

Nothing is known about the original music of the Spanish chaconne, but composers have associated it with a strictly ostinato bass which is constantly repeated many times in accompaniment to treble variations. There are four main types: minor, major, and chromatic and later with a sequence of fourths, rather like a romanesca.

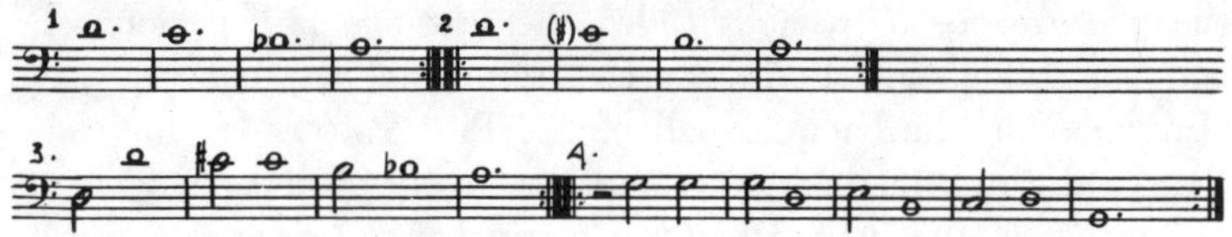

Four types of chaconne bass

The *passacaglia* also originated as a Spanish dance. Littré asserts the name came from the Spanish words *pasar* (to walk) and *calle* (street)–in other words a street song which may have been played by itinerant musicians. In an entremé, "La Escuela de Danzar," Navarrete y Ribera wrote in 1640:

> Does one wish a new dance . . . perhaps a passacalle?
> It is a type for which one is whipped,
> God preserve me from such a dangerous dance.

The passacaglias differ from chaconnes in at least five respects: 1. they are composed in minor; 2. they are slower and more stately; 3. they begin on the third beat, and more important the four- or eight-bar theme appears not only in the bass but in other parts; 5. they are never sung.

The form is very important. Eighteenth-century composers introduced it into the suite. Such organists as Buxtehude, Frescobaldi, and Bach wrote independent passacaglias to display their contrapuntal skill. Couperin, Purcell, and Handel delighted in the form. Two of the most famous are the finale of Brahms's *Fourth Symphony* and Ravel's curious interpretation in his *Bolero*.

The First Operas and the Dance

Following the death of Queen Elizabeth in 1603, which was preceded by that of Catherine de Medici in 1589, both the arts and governments saw great changes as they approached the early baroque era.

In France the throne passed to the House of Bourbon, in the person of Henry IV, who had first married Catherine's daughter, Marguerite de Valois. In 1601, he remarried Marie de Medici, niece of the great Catherine, in a lavish wedding in Florence.

Among the spectacular events presented after the nuptials was the performance of what is called the first opera. For Henry IV and his bride saw Peri's musical setting of Rinuccini's poem "Eurydice" in the banquet hall of the Pitti Palace. In this work, Peri used a new method of accompaniment for an independent solo voice, that of the figured bass for harpsichord, a style that was to exist for over a hundred years. However, the choruses were in contrapuntal style and accompanied by an orchestra made up of a voluntary group of nobles. It is notable that the custom of including a ballet in opera was established at this time. For, at the conclusion of the drama, the chorus joined in a dance which bears the directions: "*Ballo a 3, Tutto il coro insieme cantano e ballano.*"

It is interesting that dancing was even included in the so-called first oratorio, which was produced in 1600. This work derived its name from the fact that it was performed in the oratory of the Church of Sta. Maria in Vallicella, in connection with sermons and ecclesiastical functions. The steps proposed for the dances were those of the galliard, canary, and corrente.

When Marie returned to France, she brought not only the sumptuous baroque luxury, but also two prominent Italians: Rinuccini, the librettist of Eurydice, and Caccini, the composer. Thus the two countries would again mingle their artistic talents. However as time progressed it is notable that the Italians preferred the dramatic singing of opera, while the French turned to the ballet.

In France, Rinuccini studied the French *ballet comique,* and determined to introduce it to Italy. The occasion came in 1608, in connection with the festivities attendant upon two royal weddings in Italy. For the marriage of the Duke of Mantua and Infanta Margherita of Savoy, Rinuccini wrote two libretti for music composed by a now-famous young composer, Monteverdi, one-time viol player in the duke's band. The first was the tragedy *Arianna,* performed in a specially constructed theater. A few days later saw the *Ballet of the Ungrateful Ladies, Ballo delle Ungrate,* Monteverdi's most important ballet, a work modeled upon the French *ballet de cour* but in which the singers declaimed in the recitative style of the new Italian operas.

The setting represented the mouth of a wide and deep cavern. At the far end was a fiery whirlwind from which Pluto emerged to mete out a somewhat humorous retribution upon the coy and prudish ladies of Mantua who had not listened to the wooing of their lovers. The bizarre baroque mingling of spiritual and grotesque is apparent in the profound and dignified music with which Monteverdi expressed the coy ladies' bereavement for their lost beauty. The sufferings of the punished constituted the climax of the work. After the fury of this dance, the orchestra stopped, and the dancers themselves sang a four-part chorus urging the ladies of the audience to "Practice mercy, ye ladies and lasses."

The music of the ballet is written as a variation suite, wherein the main theme is a pavane which is transformed into a galliard, an allemande and a courante, followed by a repetition of the initial pavane. This type of composition was extremely popular at the time, and, although the pavane and galliard were rather old-fashioned and only infrequently performed by dancers, let it be noted that they still existed as musical styles.

Once in France, Marie de Medici revealed she was as fond of the dance as her Aunt Catherine. Undoubtedly her love for the art, as well as her fondness for dance spectacles in which she could perform, assisted the development of the court ballet. Her Majesty even composed a ballet in honor of Madame de Verneuil, which was performed by fifteen of the most beautiful ladies of the court. After the second entrée, the queen herself appeared with the favorite in the midst of the dancers. And so the lively art was revitalized under new patronage.

10

The Baroque

The baroque period began a few years before the Pilgrims landed at Plymouth Rock in 1620. It lasted almost a hundred and fifty years and included such composers as Chambonnières, Lully, Louis Couperin, Rameau, Bach, and Handel. In architecture, it appeared as a heavy and ornate style.

In 1617, Henry IV, king of France, was assassinated, and his queen, Marie de Medici, ruled for her seven-year-old son, Louis XIII. The young king warmly patronized ballets, and court life was enlivened by many dancing entertainments. In 1617, Louis XIII appeared on the stage as the *Demon du Feu* in the last and most famous of the so-called *Ballet Mélodramatiques, La Délivrance de Renault,* for which it is recorded that no fewer than sixty-four singers, twenty-four viol players, and fourteen lute players were employed to perform the music written by several court composers. A few years later, the king himself is credited with composing the music of the *Ballet de la Merlaison* (1635).

One of the most influential musical features of this period was the organization of the Twenty-four Violins of the King. They played the music for the ballets, as well as for other court entertainments. They represent the first permanent orchestra of the time and achieved international fame. For, when the orchestras of Italy and other countries were small ensembles, the *grande bande* of the king established the practice of orchestral doubling of parts to reinforce tone. It is significant that all the instruments were of the violin family. Undoubtedly, this was because their tone, which, Mersenne asserted, was more penetrating than that of the older viols, rendered them highly effective for dancers.

Meanwhile, in Italy, the opera was becoming a customary form of entertainment. A theater was made available for the first public presentation of operas when the Tron family of Venice leased their new Teatro San Cassiano to a new type of organization, a group of singers. The venture was highly successful, and opera houses soon appeared all over Italy. This brought in an entirely different audience from the invited listeners who applauded out of politeness. All sorts of people filled the boxes and balconies. Seats were taken on a first-come, first-seated basis. After the candles in the chandeliers were snuffed, young men would call the fair singers by name; they swore at others and were known to leap on the stage to express their feelings. During the entr'actes, coffee was served, vendors offered fritters, chestnuts, oranges, and other sweetmeats. Sometimes the food was not eaten, but flung at a performer who failed to please.

This public was interested in singing; it marveled at the agility of the human voice. It loved complex intrigues in the plot, disguises, assault, and murder. It adored magical, celestial appearances and miraculous scenic effects. Stage machinery was so developed that cloud-riding effects were available for the gods and angels, chariots of the sun and moon floated in the sky, and boats sailed across the stage. In time, these novelties led French cardinals and kings to import the opera to France. However the French were not like the Italians.

The French preferred action and the dance. They liked tuneful music rather than the long-lasting Italian recitatives, so filled with trills, turns, rapid scales and high notes. They complained about the length of the operas. Madame de Motteville wrote she nearly died of cold and boredom. The French preferred dancing and the dainty pantomimes of the ballet. They were fond of display and of magnificence in costume and setting. This affected the entire course of French musical entertainment. For centuries no opera was produced in France without dancing and considerable use of spectacular effects.

In France, the cardinal and statesman Mazarin sought to interest the French in Italian opera and for three years produced a new opera at carnival time, finally mounting Luigi Rossi's *Orfeo* at the amazing cost of three hundred thousand *ecus*. For this work he imported the scenic artist Torelli from Venice, where he was said to have created such mystifying stage effects that the spectators thought him in

Cinq Fées enfantent des esprits follets qui font une danse, *De Gissey, 1651, from Chalcographie du Louvre. Note fairies as part of "magical effects."* Courtesy the New York Metropolitan Museum of Art, Harris Brisbane Dick Fund, 1930

league with the Devil, and they donned masks and tried to kill him. With *Orfeo,* Torelli established a new standard in gorgeousness and installed such ingenious machinery for elaborate staging that they not only contributed to the success of this opera, but were later valuable to Lully.

In our picture, we can observe the remarkable cloud-riding fairies in the ballet of the *Fêtes de Bacchus,* performed in 1651.

The dances performed in these ballets were those performed in the ballrooms of the courtiers, with perhaps more finesse added to the branles, courantes, and gavottes of the day. The nobles were the dancers, and they were beautiful dancers, trained from early childhood by the dancing masters.

The most famous social dance introduced during the reign of Louis XIII was the *sarabande.* It quickly became an integral part of the dance suites performed in the ballrooms and played upon the clavecins and harpsichords of the salon.

The Sarabande

The sarabande, like the *chaconne,* appears to have been brought from Yucatan in Central America to the dance-hungry Spanish province of Andalusia. It is known that a native beaked flute in Guatemala was called the *zarabande.* This naming of a dance for an instrument is a common occurrence, although instruments are not named for dances. We have the tamburin, hornpipe, as well as the musette named for a French bagpipe.

Originally the Spaniards noted that the sarabande was of such a wild and primitive nature that it was banned. The Italian poet Giambattista Marino wrote, "Woe betide the dirty fellow who has brought this barbarism upon us," claiming that the girls with castanets and the men with tambourines exhibited indecency with a thousand gestures and positions, swaying their hips and knocking their breasts together, even closing their eyes and kissing while dancing the ultimate raptures of love.

The Spaniard Lope da Vega linked the sarabande and *chacona* as the same dance, while the seventeenth-century Italian dance writer Navarro maintained that the sarabande and *jacara,* as well as the *rastro* and *tarraga,* were different names for the same dance.

The sarabande is first mentioned in Europe in 1583, in a law which temporarily suppressed it in Spain, asserting that such sensuous and sexual pantomimes disgraced the Spanish nation. The law decreed that, whenever the singing and speaking of the sarabande occurred, it was to be punished with two hundred lashings and six years of hard labor for men and banishment of girls from the kingdom. In this very same year, however, a modified version of the dance was introduced to the French court of Catherine de Medici, and, although such sensuous dances as the volta and galliard were still popular, the sarabande did not become favored enough to be mentioned by Arbeau, and it had to be completely reintroduced in the next century. However, the dance was not completely suppressed in Spain. The Basle physician Thomas Platter saw it danced in Barcelona in 1599 and gives us its first dated description.

None other than the great cardinal-minister le Duc de Richelieu is credited with reintroducing the sarabande to the French court of Louis XIII when he performed it in a ballet before the queen, Anne of Austria, wearing a strange new style of trousers—wide and flowing pantaloons. These were made of green velvet and opened at both sides above garters from which dangled silver bells. Bells also tinkled on his shoes, while in his hands he clattered castanets.

Originally the sarabande had been a solo for a woman who sang to the accompaniment of a guitar as she slowly executed her steps and made graceful and suggestive use of her arms. In the courts of France and England, modified versions of the ancient sarabande were performed with a slow gliding step as a solo by a man or woman. Later, the dance was performed by couples or as a line dance with a slow and stately step and four types of figures. In England, the dance became a great favorite of Charles II, and the great English authority on dancing, Playford, noted that the English transformed it into a sort of country dance, characterized by much advancing and retiring. Four steps were taken forward and four backward while couples walked between the lines.

The music of the sarabande is slow and deliberate with a peculiar 3/4 rhythm in which the accent is placed on the second quarter of each measure.

In keeping with this syncopated figure, the music usually ends on the second and sometimes on the third beat of the bar. Mat-

Sarbande (from Handel's Almira)

theson, in *The Perfect Conductor* (1739), fitly describes the music: "The same has no other passion to express than ambition; yet therein are higher sorts to be discerned, so that the dance, sarabanda, finds itself more selected, and yet thereby a much more pompous state than the others; becsause it permits of no running notes, since the grandezza abhors such, and its severity is maintained."

The sarabande was adopted as third dance in the suite, probably by the German composer Froberger. There, its slow and dignified tempo as well as its rich harmonic texture contrasts well with the preceding allemande and courante. In time it evolved into the slow movement of the sonata and symphony. Indeed the slow movements of many symphonies by Haydn and Mozart bear a certain relationship to the old court dance.

Lully wrote some of the most effective sarabandes. Handel, in his sixth suite, wrote a sarabande with variations, while the beautiful air "Lascia ch'io pianga" from his opera *Rinaldo* was transferred almost exactly from a majestic sarabande composed as a ballet tune from a dance of Asiatics in his youthful opera, *Almira*. Evidently he favored this melody for he also used it in *Il Trionfo del Tempo.*

Bach based his famous "Goldberg Variations" on the theme of a sarabande. In more recent times, Debussy and others adopted the form. In passing, it must be observed that Corelli's sarabandes do not conform to established practices.

The Baroque

Baroque dancing was quite different from that of today. The motions were restrained and complicated, with distinctive and carefully studied motions of the hands and arms. These were the dances of an aristocratic society which had hours free to devote to the daily study of the dance. The nobility and wealthy were all trained by dance specialists from childhood. A dancing master, like the musician, was a regular member of a noble household, where he was regarded as a servant of slightly higher rank than the maids, cooks, and footmen. Louis XIV had daily lessons with his dancing master, who also trained the princes of the blood.

Dancing was such an important part of court life that it was said that one's position at court was frequently dependent on his ability on the dance floor. There were strict rules of etiquette guiding the dance.

Thus the king's grand ball was the most ceremonial of all occasions, attended by only the most influential princes and nobles. When the king wished the ball to commence, he arose, and the entire company was obliged to follow suit. Then he took his position at the end of the room near the musicians where the dancing was to begin. His partner was the queen or, in her absence, the first princess of the blood. Following them, the company ranged itself in couples according to rank and passed before the royal pair, making their bows in turn. Afterward, the king and queen opened the ball with, let us say, a branle. At the conclusion of the strain, the king and queen went to the end of the line, while the next couple led in a branle and in their turn finally took their places behind the king and queen. This procedure continued until all couples had led the dance, and Their Majesties were again at the head of the line ready to begin a courante in the same order as the branle.

Four dances customarily formed the dance suite at Versailles: the branle, courante, gavotte and minuet. Following the performance of the last, the king withdrew to the throne. When the ball was over, all couples made the same bows as at the beginning of the ball.

Most regulated balls given outside the palace strove to reproduce the atmosphere of the royal court, with a man and woman selected to play the parts of a king and queen. They began the dancing and at the conclusion of the first dance, the pseudo-queen invited another gentleman to dance with her. Even in family dances, etiquette was rigid, and partners were expected to bow and curtsey before and after dancing together.

11

Louis XIV of France

Louis xiv was a confirmed dancer and probably history's most ardent patron of the art. We know he danced in a ballet when he was only thirteen and appeared in court performances until he was thirty. Of course he played only such exalted and leading roles as Jupiter or Apollo. Indeed he was called the Sun King from a role in which he wore a heavy metal mask made to imitate the flaming rays of the sun.

The era of Louis XIV was greatly influenced by the mathematician Descartes who believed that life should be governed by the mind with mathematical precision as with a compass and ruler. This belief permeated all actions of life, etiquette, business, conversation, music, and the dance; everything was conducted formally, precisely.

Note the great palace at Versailles, which Louis XIV began to expand in 1669. Its numerous pillars, windows, wings and outbuildings are in precise, mathematical balance. Even the gardens with their fountains, paths, trees, flowers and statues are laid out in absolutely formal design.

Under Louis XIV dancing developed a distinct new style of performance, a solemn grandeur which seems singularly fitting to the broad rooms with their lofty pillars. Handel's stately sarabandes and the famous Largo bear the pompous imprint of the style. For where sixteenth-century dances had the gay upward leaps, kicks and flings of folk dances, from 1630 dancing developed a broad, sweeping, horizontal movement which seemed characteristic of the day when costumes were heavily expanded by pads and hoops.

The dancing masters fitted every dance of the new era into the step pattern of a gliding step—the plié—with a bend and a straightening of the knees, and an elevée—or rising on the toes. For almost one hundred years this elegant step with its undulating sweep was the standard for all but the marginal dances. Thus, the courante was made into a gliding dance, while the jumps of the bourrée, which had been stamped in Auvergne, were replaced with *flourets* in which there were a bending step and two concluding straight steps.

Music fell in step with the generation. The form of musical compositions became mathematically precise with neat little dance melodies written in perfectly balanced phrases of four, eight, twelve, or sixteen measures. Along with the broadening effects of artistic style and also following the change in the succession of dance steps to the three movements of bend, lift, and glide, lay an expansion of the musical time elements, as in the courante, where two measures of 3/4 meter were rendered into one measure of 6/4. This practice had already appeared in the sixteenth-century galliard where the fourth step of one group became the first beat of the second measure, and by this the rhythmic pattern of the dance and its music took on the characteristic of the so-called *hemiola,* which is imbedded in the French courante.

1 2 3 | 1 2 3

3/4 ♩ ♩ ♩ | ♩ ♩ ♩ |

Galliard L R L R *Leap*

Minuet *Bend* | *Bend* | L R

Courante

6/4 ♩ ♩ | ♩ ♩ | ♩ ♩ |

Louis XIV—Hemiola rhythms

To codify rules of artistic perfection, the French formed academies for each art, and their members were invited to draw up their own regulations. The Academy of the Dance was first organized between 1661 and '63. The king's approval in 1662 enabled dancing masters to teach without a master's certificate and as independent artists.

Louis XIV was delighted with the organization since it helped make his courtiers better dancers, not only by improving their "lamentable" incompetence, but also by training a greater number

Figure 1. *The First Position*

Figure 2. *The Second Position*

Figure 3. *The Fourth Position*

Figure 4. *The Fifth Position*

Maître à danser, *Rameau, circa 1725*

to perform in court ballets, for in those days, only nobles appeared in court performances. The court's chief dancing instructor, Beauchamps, soon became the first director of the Royal Academy of Dancing.

From the Academy of the Dance came a systematic organization of the art, reduced to a few very narrow rules, founded upon the principles of the five positions, which were devised to give the dancer a secure and complete balance whichever way he moved. Thus, in this period, even the physical motions of the dance were reduced to mathematical fundamentals which classically emphasized static qualities rather than movements. In this art, the study of technique became all important.

In addition, the dancers performed a highly elaborate use of the arms, wrists, and hands which was applied to all court dances. These furnished some of the most prettily expressive features of all baroque dancing. Dancers of medium height were advised to raise their arms no higher than the pits of their stomachs, since if they were higher the posture not only tended to be stiff and ungraceful, but also resembled a cross. Short persons were an exception and were advised to raise their arms higher in order to appear taller. Ladies were taught to hold their voluminous skirts between their thumbs and first fingers with the hands daintily turned outward, and with arms so extended at the sides that they neither spread nor squeezed the dresses.

There were three different movements for the arms and three similar movements for the wrists, elbows, and shoulders with hands facing up or down. The actions of the wrists and hands were enhanced by the elegant embroidered cuffs with their frothy lace and fluttering ribbons, which set off the dainty gestures as a frame enhances a picture. Dancing masters sought to correlate these motions with those of the legs, following the principles of the normal action of walking, whereby a forward motion of the right foot is balanced by a backward motion of the left hand.

The most exciting period of the reign of Louis XIV began in 1661 when at the age of twenty-three, he took over the government. It lasted until 1683. In this period, Louis won his greatest victories and his court shone with such dazzling radiance that all the kings and princes of Europe wanted to imitate him and recreate their courts in the manner of the great Sun King. During this time his court became a veritable fairyland with days crowded with entertainments vying in magnificence. Now it became necessary for everyone of any importance to study the dance since success at court practically depended on one's ability as a dancer. When we think of the composers of the period, of Lully, Couperin, and others, we think of their relationship to the dance.

The *courante* was one of Louis XIV's favorite dances, and he is said to have excelled his entire court in performing it. This might be expected since it is recorded that for twenty-two years he practiced it for a few hours daily with the court dancing masters. Falling

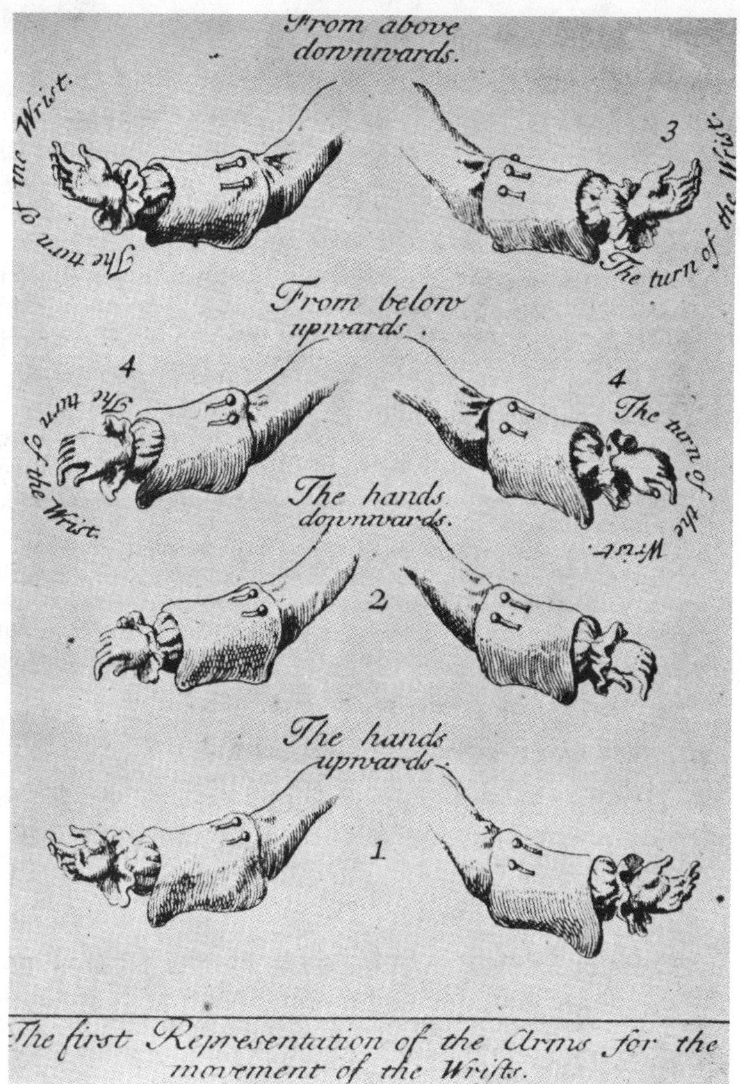

The First Represeṅtation of the Arms for the Movement of the Wrists, *from Rameau's* Maître à danser, *Paris*, 1725

The Courante

in line with their ruler, courtiers found it was absolutely essential to learn the movements of the courante. Also, since the dance was simpler and slower than other dances, it was among the first learned.

The courante was first mentioned in 1515 as a lively folklike French dance. Arbeau described it as follows:

> When I was young, the courante took the form of a game or ballet; three young men chose three girls, and placing themselves in a row, the first danced with his partner, then led her to the other side of the room, returning alone to his companions; the second did the same; then the third, leaving the three girls by themselves. When the third had returned, the first, gamboling and making all kinds of amorous glances, pulling up his hose and straightening his shirt, went to claim his damsel. She refused him, turning her back upon him. The young man then returned to his place pretending despair. The two others did the same. At last all went together to their damsels, each to his own, kneeling down and begging with clasped hands for mercy. The three damsels then yielded and all danced the courante pell-mell. . . . While they dance, they often make turns, releasing the damsel's hand; then after the turn, they take it again and go on. When a dancer's companions observe he is weary, they go and steal his damsel and dance with her themselves.

During the two centuries of its popularity, the courante varied to suit changing tastes. The pantomime was dropped, then the prescribed steps, but the speed was retained and even Shakespeare mentions "swift corantos" in 1600. Indeed *courante* is French for "running."

The folklike character disappeared in the elegant court of Louis XIV. Now dancing masters formulated strict rules for its performance. Dancers first made the customary double bow or curtsey, one forward and one backward, then presented hands and commenced a set figure utilizing the new gliding step of the era and a *pas de courante.*

Composers delighted in the dance since it first appeared and there are many examples extant. These have differed in rhythm in various countries. Arbeau's example in 4/4 time is unusual since others are usually in triple meter.

The Italian corrente or coranto has rapid runs in sixteenth notes.

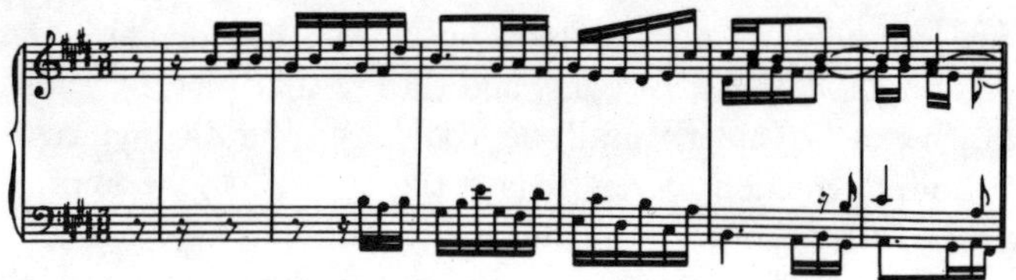

Italian courante (from Handel's "First Ordre #5")

The true French court dance shows a preference for fairly slow dotted rhythms.

French courante (from Matheson's "Suite II")

Another variety appears to have been developed from the others by musicians who seem to have been particularly pleased by the opportunity to use cross accents by dividing the 6/4 rhythm so that it had three beats per measure as in 3/2 and also the two accents of 6/4 which usually occurred in the last bar of a section. This is known as the antique style of so-called hemiola rhythm. Our example is from Couperin's "Suite in G minor."

Courante (from Couperin's "Suite in G minor")

After learning the courante, dancers began to learn the minuet.

The Minuet

The minuet was devised for Louis XIV. Its popularity lasted for one hundred and fifty years, and during that time no courtier's education was complete until he could perform the dance with grace and distinction. Even today, the music of the minuet is played in homes, concerts and broadcasts, although the dance itself is not performed due to changes in dress and manners as well as difficulty in performance.

The minuet sprang from the rustic branle de Poitou, in which girls lightly raised their wooden shoes and clattered on the floor. Arbeau adds that they stamped on the second and third bars of triple time.

Air of the "Branle de Poitou" (from Arbeau)

This was a chain dance performed by many people following the steps of their leaders until the head couple detached themselves and danced down the line, facing the other dancers. At the end, the cavalier turned his lady so that they could form a new line, or join at the bottom of the first line, thus completing an S curve, which the other dancers followed in turn.

It is said that Louis XIV first danced a minuet, in 1663, to music written by his favorite composer and contemporary, Lully. The king was then twenty-five years old. The court dancing master, Beauchamps, appears to have designed the small, mincing steps of the dance, which took its name from the French *menu,* meaning small. The first minuets were very simple, but, under the influence of baroque trends, the dance masters completely altered the form.

Lully's first minuet bears a decided resemblance to Arbeau's branle, which is divided into two sections, each containing nine

Lully's first minuet (from Schubart's Aesthetic der Tunkunst, *1806)*

beats or nine measures. For his minuet, Lully used three phrases, each of which is clearly divided into three measures, then repeated. The second portion of the music is quite different, containing two, distinct, four-measure phrases, revealing that Lully had already begun those alterations which changed the entire dance and music.

The beauty of the dance and the difficulty of the steps made the minuet quite an event for each couple, especially since it was performed with the floor cleared of other dancers. Actually the minuet was a spectacular art dance, the result of diligent practice, for which some studied as long as six years before public performance.

The main point of the dance was the floor pattern, which followed the letter Z. Partners stood at opposite ends of the letter, facing each other, then moved two *pas de menuet* to the left, two *pas* passing each other on the diagonal, and two more in which both partners moved to the right. Each *pas* required six beats of music, or two measures, with an accent on the first beat of the first measure. Musicians were advised not to accent the second measure. The Z could be repeated or varied when the partners gave right or left hands and turned in a circle.

The Z figure cleverly made the performers visible on all sides of the audience, in front, on the side, in profile and in back. It was particularly charming since the lady was able to display all the beauty of her person and her grace, as well as the splendor of her rich gown with its spreading skirt. Her charm was further heightened by the artful manner with which she opened her fan as she trod the graceful figures of the dance.

The minuet represents a sublimation of the wooing pantomime. It was a disciplined ritual wherein partners touched hands only in the brief moment of passing.

One feature of the music is the so-called *trio,* which follows the first part of the music with a contrasting melody, after which the first portion is repeated. The origin of this may be found in Lully's works. In his operas, one minuet is followed by another in a single act, for evidently the dance was so popular that neither the dancers nor the audience was satisfied with one minuet. Most likely this practice developed into the *trio* or *da capo* form so named because the second section was sometimes written in three-part harmony and intended for three instruments.

Lully's minuets have no trios, but often designate *Première* and *Deuxième* menuet. However, they do feature contrasts. Frequently the first minuet was sung, while the second was played by instruments and intended for dancing. Often the first minuet was then repeated.

The seventeenth-century minuet was rather slow and stately, but, as time went on, dancing masters invented more and more variations, and the dance became quicker. However it must be remembered that the *pas de menuet* required two full measures with the steps so divided that they were carried over the first bar line. In his *Dictionnaire de la danse,* Compan wrote, "The number of measures must be four or a multiple thereof, for this is necessary due to the execution of the *pas de menuet*. And care should be taken by the musicians to emphasize each division by a noticeable drop in the music, in order to aid the ear of the dancer and keep him in time."

When the dance suite lost popularity, shortly after the time of Bach, the minuet achieved a new immortality by being included in the symphony. In its new surroundings, the minuet gained a new lilt, a rustic freedom that comes from the folk. Haydn, Mozart and the young Beethoven gave it increasing speed and a sound of the Alps, the *Ländler,* and the new waltz. Eventually Beethoven felt the old dance smacked of the old regime and was not at all democratic. His minuets were rougher and quicker. Eventually he bustled it off into the form of a scherzo.

The Rigadoon

The *rigaudon* or *rigadoon* was another lively dance enjoyed by Louis XIV. This sprightly dance originated in Provence or Languedoc, where it was sung and danced to the rhythmic accompaniment of the tambourine. According to tradition, it derived its name from the dancing master Rigaud, who introduced it in Paris during the reign of Louis XIII. However, Curt Sachs feels the name may be related to the Italian *rigadone–rigolone*–and its diminutive, *rigoletto* (circle dance).

There was much hopping, running and turning in the dance, while *balancés* were made with small quick steps. The skillful dancers of the French court were delighted by its frolicsome gaiety and liked to interpolate many virtuoso steps into their performances. The possibility for interpolation as well as its light, feathery steps made it well suited to the virtuoso ballet dancer. For this reason it continued its existence on the stage long after its lack of sedateness caused its popularity to wane in the ceremonious ballrooms of later years.

"Rigaudon en Rondeau" (from Rameau's Dardanus*)*

The music of the rigaudon is light and brittle, filled with runs and light staccato notes. It begins on the fourth beat of lively 2/4 or 4/4 time which is subdivided into many eighth notes, each of which was transformed into a step by the ballet dancers; even the "upbeat," with which the music commenced, was subdivided. Rameau wrote two of the finest examples, one of which is included in his opera *Dardanus*.

12

Lully and the Spectacular Dance

INTO THE GLITTERING and music-loving atmosphere surrounding the youthful king, Louis XIV, stepped young Jean-Baptiste Lully, only five years older than his sovereign. Being a clever dancer and mimic, a ready composer of dance music to the royal taste, and also an excellent conductor, he rapidly gained a position of great importance.

Lully was an Italian, born near Florence in 1633. There, despite his lack of systematic musical training, his talent for playing the guitar attracted the attention of the Chevalier de Guise, who brought him to Paris, where his sponsors enabled him to study violin and, probably, dancing. In 1653 he danced five roles in the *Ballet de la Nuite* and possibly composed some of the music. This attracted the attention of young Louis XIV, then about fifteen years of age, and the young musician was quickly admitted to the king's band of violins. Before long, and when barely out of his teens, he became the director of a special *bande des petits violons*, consisting of sixteen and later twenty-one violins. These were carefully drilled in the dry and pointed style of absolute rhythmic precision which eventually became admired and imitated all over Europe. Undoubtedly this characteristic orchestra discipline assisted his later superiority in the field of ballet, for dance accompaniment needs precision and rhythmic definiteness.

In 1658, Lully made his name by writing the music for *Alcidiane* to the words of Benserade. This began his association with the great writers of the period, and he was commissioned to write music for Molière's comedy-ballets. At this time, Mazarin, the cardinal-minister, was making arrangements to celebrate the marriage of Louis XIV. The Venetian composer Cavalli was engaged to present a new opera in a luxurious new theater to be built in the

Tuileries and designed with the latest mechanical contrivances by the Italian Gasparo Vigarini.

Unfortunately Mazarin died in 1661 without seeing Cavalli's *Ercole Amante* performed at the festivities of 1662. This spectacle outshone all previous operas and lasted fully six hours, much of which time was consumed by the huge ballets which Lully was engaged to prepare in the French manner for the end of each act. Indeed, Lully pushed himself so far that the work was not viewed as a music drama with inserted ballets, but as a gigantic ballet with inserted dramatic operatic incidents. The French seem to have been quite indifferent to Cavalli's fine score. However, they may not have heard the tunes on account of the clatter of the huge machines carrying down the cloud effects (*les gloires*) containing some one hundred and fifty singers and dancers!

Following Mazarin's death, attempts to introduce Italian opera ended. The new minister favored musical nationalism, and Lully ardently supported French music. His ballets assumed increasing importance, and he soon commenced his association with the great actor-dramatist Molière from which sprang the *comédies-ballets* of Lully's second phase of ballet writing. The collaboration was accidental, for, while writing *Les Facheux* in 1661, Molière decided to insert a few danced entrées between the scenes while the actors were changing costumes. His dramatic instinct rejected the idea of inserting unrelated dances; hence he merged dance, music, and clever words into a combination which he wrote was "new to our stage although one might find authority for it in antiquity . . . and it may serve as a suggestion for other performances which can be worked out at further leisure."

In 1664, Lully began his fruitful partnership with Molière in *Le Mariage Forcé,* in which Lully himself danced a supporting role. The première dancer of this production was the great Beauchamps, who also served as the choreographer, for which he received fifty gold louis. The danced interludes of the work were so prominent that they almost eclipsed Molière's dialogue and comedy. Another new feature was Lully's replacement of the recitation of the old *ballet de cour* with songs sung by professional singers.

Thus a new era in the ballet began. For instead of mere suites of dances by various composers employing several costumers, scene

Seconde Journée: Théatre fait dans la mesme allée, fur lequel la Comédie, et le Ballet de la Princesse d'Elide, furent representez, *from the Chalcographie du Louvre. This is from Lully's ballet.* Courtesy the New York Metropolitan Museum of Art, Harris Brisbane Dick Fund, 1930

painters and choreographers and tied by a vague plot, Lully's works had one composer and musical director with the dance episodes unified by a single purpose. Further, Lully was assisted by the greatest decorators, dance directors, and such literary geniuses as Benserade, Molière, Corneille, and Racine.

Lully also developed the almost new feature in ballet-writing of musical stylization. His dances have a certain ability to indicate farce and mood, as in the soft music provided for the "pale shades" of *Proserpine*. Furthermore he revealed his first-hand knowledge of the musical needs of a dancer: they are graceful, rhythmic, and only simply contrapuntal. True, he used the rhythms of the court dances: bourrées, passepieds, canaries, and later the gigue. However, these may not have been performed as in the ballroom. Prunières insists that they were usually composed by the professional choreographers from the Ballet de la Maison. It is asserted that it took fifteen days of rehearsal to prepare a *grand* ballet and eight days to produce a *petit* ballet.

These ballets, however, might seem boring today, more like elegant marching than dancing, for the dancers were usually courtiers whose actions were impeded by stiff and elaborate court costumes with long wide skirts projected out upon wires, with male attire amplified by wigs and high heels, not to mention the elaborate metal armor and headdresses required for representation of mythological and classical personages.

Professionals gradually began to take over on the stage after Louis XIV suddenly stopped his stage appearances. The nobles followed the royal example and left the field entirely in the hands of trained dancers. At first, women did not dance on the stage, and boys, wearing masks, enacted female parts. But in 1681 Lully introduced the first ballerina, Mademoiselle La Fontaine, in *Le Triomphe de l'Amore*! She was soon followed by Mademoiselles Subligny and Maupin. From then on, women gradually took over, until men were almost entirely replaced.

Meanwhile, attempts were made to produce a national opera in France, and the composer Perrin persuaded Colvert to grant him the royal patent for the sole right to produce such a work. In 1671, Perrin and Cambert opened the Académie Royale du Musique et de la Danse with the first real French opera, *Pomone*, with great success. Lully now stepped in and wrested the royal patent from Perrin, who was in prison, and he contrived to secure a new patent by 1672. This gave Lully complete monopoly over the opera and all theatrical music as well as all the money derived from his music for himself and his heirs. Thus he became the absolute ruler of French music from which position he amassed one of the largest fortunes ever derived from the art of music. He produced a new opera every year, in addition to his ballets, until his death in 1687.

Among his responsibilities for this work was the reform of the young Académie de la Danse which he turned over to his trusted colleague, Beauchamps, the king's dancing master and perhaps the first great French dancer. He and his successors, Pécour and, later, Feuillet, so firmly established the basis for virtuoso technique that the names of the positions of the classic dance are still learned in French all over the world.

None of Lully's colleagues or successors was able to surpass him, not even his pupil Colasse, who reportedly helped score his works. For a while, Italian composers took over, and their characteristic interest in singing probably wrought musical changes. We now find that the best French music began to appear in the smaller scale of the salon concert. Soon evidences of the new Rococo style became evident in the pastel nuances of Couperin's compositions.

An interesting development in answer to the need of preserving dance motion, particularly those of stage dancers, was the work of Raoul Le Feuillet, Beauchamps's pupil, who is credited with the first dance notation (the *chorégraphie* in 1699) since the fifteenth century. His plates indicate the position of the feet and the floor pattern executed by them, while various steps and leaps were indicated by special signs. This choreography was designed for the floor plan of the stage dance. And the fact that it does not consider the motions of the trunk, head and arms reveals the horizontal aspect of baroque dancing.

These horizontal patterns were frequently traced on the floor of the stage, and dancers even followed the wavy patterns and geometric figures. These patterns were also used in great military maneuvers and especially for the equestrian ballets.

Note our illustration from Kellon Tomlinson's *Art of Dancing,* printed in 1735.

Illustration from Kellon Tomlinson's Art of Dancing, *1735. Presenting both arms at the conclusion of minuet. The figures drawn at the feet in a circular arabesque are the notations of a dancing master to describe the motions of the dance.* Courtesy Dance Collection, The New York Public Library at Lincoln Center (Gift of Lincoln Kirstein)

In it we see the dancers presenting both arms at the conclusion of a minuet. The figures, drawn at the feet of the dancers in a circular arabesque, are the notations by which dancing masters preserved and described the motions of dancers.

Salon Music in the Era of Louis XIV

Louis XIV lived virtually his whole life to the accompaniment of music. He had music when dining, when at church, when playing cards. Undoubtedly he heard Lully's airs played by his soldiers as they marched to battle. In his private apartments, composers showed him the music they were writing for the ballet and opera. He even suggested subjects for new operas and ballets. The king played the guitar and harpsichord; he sang very agreeably and even composed. The royal family were all taught to play musical instruments by Lully and other famous composers.

There were a number of specifically musical functions at court, such as the numerous *petits concerts* at which Lully and, later, Couperin himself performed. The salon concert was well established, and many of Lully's airs and ballet tunes were arranged for these events. The master composed a number of special pieces for such occasions. Of course the aristocracy followed the example of their rulers, thus creating a certain demand for music.

In this salon music, French composers seem to have captured the charming characteristics of the time, the polished ceremony, the measured grace. These composers did not aim at grand effects or a display of contrapuntal subtlety, but simply had a desire to please the ear with pretty tunes.

The harpsichord was the favored key instrument. It had various names in different countries, such as the *clavecin* in France and the *clavicembalo* in Italy. Back in 1464 it was mentioned as a *clavicymbalum* by the Minnesingers. Since it could not sustain harmony, it called into being a sort of flickering accompaniment, requiring a brilliant style, filled with quickly strummed arpeggios and scales.

The French were the first to realize the possibilities of the instrument and they seized upon the idea of the suite, based on dance forms, which they grouped into collections called *ordres*. In the early years of Louis XIV, Jacques de Chambonnières was the foremost composer, and he is called the father of the school. He published two books of dances in 1670 of which several sets are arranged in the most orthodox fashion of allemande, courante, sarabande, and perhaps a gigue. He also gave the directions for executing the embellishments which are the most characteristic features of harpsichord music. However, like his predecessor, Gaultier, his pieces also bore such fanciful titles as "Iris," "La Toute Belle," and "La Dunkerque." Many are also called *tombeaus* (tombs) and are sort of memorial pieces for a friend. They are in the form of an allemande.

François Couperin was the most famous harpsichord composer of the day, and, more than any other composer, he established the suite as the most fashionable type of music for domestic performance. Born in 1668 into a family of musicians, he rose into the favor of Louis XIV a few years after the death of Lully and eventually won from the king his own title, "*Le Grand.*"

The little concerts of the king were charming occasions which Louis XIV is said to have enjoyed nearly as much as the opera. One can imagine the colorful group of great ladies and noble courtiers gathered in one of the magnificent salons of Versailles. Here they sat with self-conscious dignity upon the cushions of the carved and gold-backed chairs, beneath the light of the golden candelabra, carrying on their gracious conversations and love affairs as they attentively listened to the silvery music played by the court clavicinist, Couperin, who sat erectly before his clavecin, with his plump features carefully composed beneath an imposing wig. Now and then he glanced at members of the audience to see if they understood the implications of the title of the composition. For, although his pieces were in the dance forms, many bore such titles as "La- Majesteure," "L'Enchantress," and "L'Ingénue" and were either dedicated to, or musical portraits of, the great ladies of the court. Other pieces were programmatic or descriptive, such as "The Spinners," "The Hunt," or "The Man with the Grotesque Body."

Couperin's fame spread far beyond France. His influence upon Bach is observable in fingering, ornaments and content. Bach also adopted the rhythmic oddities of such dances as the courantes.

England was not far behind France in the cultivation of the harpsichord, and, when Charles II returned in 1660 with the Restoration of the Stuarts, there was a wave of French dances and customs. For Charles II was the grandson of Henry IV of France and had been educated there, where he had heard the music of Lully's youth. Moreover, Cromwell and the Commonwealth had prohibited dancing, and the old English dances had disappeared. Finally the famous Beau Nash became known as the master of the pump room at Bath and English dances were absolutely banished when Bath became the center of fashion. Most society followed his dictum and studied the French dances.

The English had become very fond of private music in their homes. All aristocrats and well-to-do families took lessons from private teachers. For their study there were numerous publications for such performance. The English appropriately called their suites "lessons." For the most part, these followed the same order of dances as the French *ordres*. The finest English composer was Purcell; he had great originality and a daring which surpassed even the French composers. His operas and sonatas reveal great charm and mastery. Another famous English composer was John Blow. These were the last two great English composers for decades. True, Handel brought a great period to England, but he came from Germany.

English society was far different from the French. The Puritan uprising had created a well-to-do middle class who became patrons of the arts. Amateur music societies sprang up all over England. Enterprising businessmen soon started to cater to the new interest, and the first regular concerts for paying audiences were initiated between 1672 and 1678. These developed into the so-called coal-house concerts held in Thomas Briton's loft, which were reached by a crazy flight of steps erected beside his coal stable. An astonishing array of listeners, including members of elegant society, attended these Thursday events to hear Pepusch and even Handel.

Much later, in 1732, Jonathan Tyrse opened Vauxhall Gardens on the banks of the Thames. The cream of London society flocked here to dine and hear the finest musicians available. One usually hired a boat to reach these brilliant pleasure gardens, which shone at night across the black waters of the Thames in the gleaming splendor from a thousand lamps. Here, in a setting fit for a king, one could sup in a fascinating box and hear a dainty minuet of Handel or excerpts from an opera.

Handel also had royal patronage. Three years after his German patron, the Elector of Hanover, was crowned King George I of England, the king commissioned him to write music to be performed on a barge as he floated down the Thames. This suite of twenty-one pieces, including dance forms, is known as the "Water Music." Later, the king commissioned music to be performed as part of a great celebration for the signing of the peace of Aix-la-

Vauxhall Gardens. Courtesy the New York Metropolitan Museum of Art, Harris Brisbane Dick Fund, 1917

Chapelle. Since fireworks were part of the festivities, the music is known as the "Fireworks Music." It consists of an overture and five movements, including a bourrée and two minuets. A tremendous orchestra of fifty-six brass and woodwinds was engaged for the public rehearsal in Vauxhall Gardens. This was attended by such a crowd that traffic on London Bridge was held up for three hours.

Meanwhile, in Germany, Bach accepted the post of *Kappelmeister* to Prince Leopold of Anhalt-Cothen in the year George I heard the "Water Music." The prince was fond of collecting the secular music of Vivaldi, Corelli, and Purcell, as well as the German Froberger and Muffat. Here, Bach had the opportunity to see the work of other composers. In addition, the dancing master taught in a nearby building, and the two had ample opportunity to exchange ideas.

Here, Bach composed many of his compositions in the dance forms; many were written for actual dancing. However, it is interesting to note that, whereas Handel wrote for kings, princes and, more important, the new wider public, Bach wrote most of his dances for his immediate circle. He wrote many for the music study of his wife, his children and his pupils. Of course, many were performed at the salon concerts of the court, and his larger works were for courtly audiences and some public performances. In 1723, Bach accepted the post of cantor at St. Thomas Church in Leipzig and began the production of his vast number of sacred compositions. However, late in life, he brought forth such great secular works as the English suites and the partitas.

The Sonata Form

A great achievement of early baroque composers was the establishment of instrumental styles and forms. The problems of writing longer instrumental compositions were greatly alleviated by the writers of the dance forms. From their custom of grouping contrasting dances together were developed the longer cyclic forms of the suite and the sonata.

In Italy, the earlier types of cyclic compositions were in the form of the *canzona,* a musical form with several short sections of sharply different rhythms, often in dance styles. However, these were not detached from each other. Thus in a *canzona* of Giovanni Battista Grillo, the first section contains only seven measures; the second has eleven measures in the style of a galliard; the third is in the contrapuntal style of a ricercar; the fourth is like a pavane, the fifth a galliard, and so forth.

The development of the violin in the early seventeenth century was very influential in advancing the style of purely instrumental composition. The Italians first became interested in the violin when a number of families in northern Italy perfected the instrument, including Maggini, the Amatis (1596-1684), Guarneri and finally Antonio Stradivari, who lived until 1737. Fascinated by this instrument, a great group of Italian violinists and composers developed a style of composition which could display their technical virtuosity as well as the possibilities of the instrument.

Possibly Giovanni Legrenzi (1625-1690) was one of the most gifted of these early composers. He separated the little sections of the *canzonas* by pauses and thus produced a composition of four distinct movements. By the middle of the century this developed into a style called a *sonata da camera,* an instrumental work for chamber performance using dance forms. Another style was the *sonata da chiesa,* literally "church sonata" which omitted the use of dance titles, since dance music was not permitted in the church, but which was animated by dance rhythms. Thus the last *sonata da chiesa* of a set published by Legrenzi in 1655 opens with a fugue, followed by a dignified movement in a style similar to a sarabande, and a third movement is a short "adagio," which is followed by a lively "finale."

Giovanni Battista Vitali is credited with giving the *sonata da chiesa* its definite form in a collection published in 1667, where we find combinations of dances in suites evolving into the sonata form. Through such works and following the perfection of the violin, composers gradually developed the sonata with movements bearing only tempi indications, except, perhaps, for the inclusion of a minuet, which briefly reveals the dance ancestry of the form.

The Country Dance, *engraving by W. Hogarth*

13

The English Country Dances

Square Dancing

The American square dances are the descendants of the English country dance called *contredanse* in France and were brought to America by the colonists.

Springing from the ancient round dances and rustic chain dances, which had long flourished among the English country folk, they were a part of the merrymaking on the village green, bridals and fairs being enjoyed whenever there was an opportunity for dancing.

Like many folk dances, these everyday country dances were based on the sex motif and performed by couples with every figure and evolution related to symbolic portrayal of flirtation and coquetry. The sexes were separated and danced toward each other, performers holding hands and dancing about together; sometimes they kissed.

The country dances were not long the exclusive property of the English country folk. They went from the village green to the fashionable drawing room. At the court of Queen Elizabeth, in 1602, the Earl of Worcester wrote to the Earl of Salisbury that, "we all frolic here at Court, much dancing in the Privy Chamber of country dances before the Queen's Majesty who is exceedingly pleased therewith."

However, it must be noted that the energetic country dances did not compete with the more elegant courantes, galliards, and other French dances, either in the court or refined society. These latter were performed in the earlier part of the evening, while lighter forms of amusement were desired later.

During the reign of James I, when the court began to rebel at the formality of French dances, country dances acquired greater favor, and it was said that it was easier to put on fine clothes than learn French dances.

The country dances continued to be popular during the seventeenth century, even in spite of the temporary prohibition of dancing by the Puritans, and they quickly reappeared after the Restoration. Samuel Pepys observed King Charles II dancing them in 1662 and wrote, "The King led a lady in a single coranto, and then the rest of the lords, one after another, other laides: very noble it was, and a great pleasure to see. Then to country dances, the King leading the first, which he called for, which was, says he 'Cuckolds all Awry, the old dance of England." Yet the new regime saw a slight abatement in the popularity of country dances at fashionable assemblies where dancing was more reserved and ceremonious.

However, by the end of the century, the English country dances began to challenge the supremacy of the more formal court dances, and they appeared on the Continent. References state that the Duke of Monmouth taught them to Dutch ladies at The Hague in 1685. Indeed the French court sent the famous dancing master Isaac d'Orléans to study country dances in England, while, in 1688 the Parisian dancing master Landrin wrote that he had gone to England three years earlier to secure new *contres* for the dauphin and had collected the rarest ones at the school from which Isaac d'Orléans had secured his *contres*. Strangely, while the dances were blooming in France, they were losing their popularity in England.

The country dances were compiled and published in the *English Dancing Master* (1650-51), by John Playford. The book was printed and reprinted; new tunes and dances were constantly added until the original modest collection of about a hundred dances increased to a thousand.

This is a very strange dance book, for, whereas huge manuals were written about how to dance a minuet, no directions describe how to dance country dances. They were passed down from generation to generation. Apparently only the tunes plus the figures of chain round, promenade, wheel, or weave figures, which sprang from old rites, were necessary. Originally the tunes were played by a piper who accompanied himself with the ancient tabor—a small drum—suspended upon his little finger. The combination sounded very sweet, especially when the dances were performed on the green lawns of England. The dances were performed as one wished, in march, hop, skip, walk, waltz, or polka step.

Under the melodies of the Playford Collection are two types of symbols which stem from the Neolithic Age. A sun represents a man, while a moon represents a lady. The accompanying directions indicate such actions as: "suns forth, moons back," or "join hands forth and back." Country dances were performed by equal numbers of men and women, each requiring no fewer than six persons.

The *English Dancing Master* contains two general types of choral dance: rounds and longways. The round is actually the old French branle, that is, a circle dance with alternating men and women. In the longways, the men face the women in parallel lines and sometimes advance with sprightly and jaunty steps until they meet, then bow and retire. Sometimes the first, second, and third men on one side advance toward the first, second, and third women until they meet, taking two steps to each bar for two bars, after which they move back, returning to their former places.

Almost every figure requires eight measures of music for completion, and most figures are repeated over and over while each couple performs in turn. Because of the variety of tunes and figures, it became customary for the leading couple to have the "call" or privilege of naming the tunes and figures they wished to dance. To modern ears, the leader might sound droll as he called the quaint titles of the airs, "Now, lads, take your partners for 'The Bath,' or for 'The Ladies' Misfortune,' for 'Tails All,' for 'Under and Over,' or for 'The Slaughterhouse.' "

Some directions for the dances sound equally amusing. Thus, the lovely old dance tune "All in a Garden Green," which Byrd used for a series of variations, states that, after three couples had arranged themselves lengthwise and performed a few figures, the "first man shake his own 'wo' by the hand, then 2 [second], then 3 by one hand, then by the other, kiss her twice, turn her, shake her by the hand, then the 2, then your own by one hand, then by the other, kiss her twice, and turn her, . . ."

Historians had considerable confusion regarding the origin of the dances. Even in America there have been various names of square dances, folk dances, and so forth. There is also the *cotillon.*

Germany varied the French title calling their version a *Contretanze.*

When Mozart visited Prague in 1787 to view the performance of his opera *Figaro* during the carnival season, he attended the famous Bretfield Ball, where he observed the performance of contretanzes which he described in a letter to his friend Jaquin, in Vienna.

"I was highly pleased to watch all those people dance to my music from *Figaro,* transformed into contretanzes and Germans [allemandes], and they hopped around with great pleasure."

Mozart himself rewrote "Non Piu Andrai" as a contretanze and in the year of his death (1791) included it as a first in his group of five contre dances. In 1801 Beethoven published a set of twelve contretanzes for orchestra in lively 2/4 time and used two of these in the finale of his ballet *Prometheus.*

14

The Rococo Period

FOLLOWING THE DEATH of Louis XIV in 1715, the pompous grandeur of the baroque with its classical formalism, gradually merged into the Rococo, a period named from the word *rocaille* (shell), a term originally referring to the period's charming and artificial little rock gardens connected by narrow lanes lined with pebbles. Rococo style was purely decorative; the shell motif appeared everywhere, along with festoons of garlands and chubby cherubs.

This was a feminine style, and the youthful Louis XVI soon showed his preference for feminine society with his royal mistresses, Mmes Du Barry and Pompadour. Extravagant dress fashions undoubtedly bore their imprint on dancing. Men adopted lace ruffles, embroidery, powdered wigs and sweeping plumes; from 1718 women's skirts were extended by panniers until they eventually reached the enormous circumference of eighteen feet, while trains further impeded movement. By 1745, these proved so cumbersome to dancers that ladies were in danger of tripping and falling when they turned or tried to move backwards. To prevent such an incident, the celebrated dance master Marcel invented *un coup de talon* (a kick with the heel) and a sidestep. This proved to be difficult, for the laws of good taste dictated that the upper part of the body should not show the slightest movement.

During the early days of the regency of Louis XV, opera balls were inaugurated. Eventually they gained such popularity that three were given each night throughout the carnival season. These fetes were presented in the auditorium of the Opera in luxurious magnificence. The orchestra was divided, with fifteen musicians at each end of the room. A half-hour before the ball, the musicians gave a concert in the octagon room, performing compositions of the best masters. In the ensuing ball the room reeled in confusion, everyone danced and swirled together, all ranks and professions, great ladies and adventurers; everyone wore a mask. Thus even Louis XV was unrecognized when he attended in 1737.

The elegant minuet was favored. However the rapid passepied and the lively gavotte achieved new triumphs. The allemande also reappeared briefly as a figure dance, but was soon remembered as a step in the country dance, and the term "to allemande" meant to turn your partner with arms interlaced, usually with one arm behind the back.

Every dance master of repute devised his own version of the minuet. These were more difficult than the old *menuet de la cour,* and each was accompanied by special music so that the musicians might conclude at the same time as the dancers. Compan, in his *Dictionary of the Dance* (1787) adds that "The number of measures must be four or a multiple thereof, for this is necessary to the execution of the Pas de Menuet."

The zenith of the Rococo occurred with the accession of Louis XVI and Marie Antoinette in 1774; then fashion, decoration and court life reached new excesses. Hoop skirts reached unbelievable width, and headdresses reached such heights that ladies were seen kneeling in their carriages or riding with their heads extended out the windows. Marie Antoinette loved to sing and dance. In Vienna, the great Gluck had been her music teacher, and Noverre had taught her dancing.

The gavotte became a favorite dance after the queen heard a minuet which the composer Gretry had written to the air of a gavotte. From the union of the two dances, one in 3/4 time, one in 4/4, resulted the so-called *menuet de la reine* after the queen, who supposedly danced it to perfection. This slow gavotte was a far cry from the rustic dance of the Gaps. Eventually Gretry composed another favorite gavotte, and such composers as Gluck soon followed.

Toward the middle of the century, a new philosophy of life appeared, advocating a return to nature. The leader was the Swiss Jean Jacques Rousseau (1712-1778), who became the guide, philosopher and friend of fashionable society. The queen became so enamored of his philosophy that she built a pseudo-farm at Versailles, Le Petit Trianon, where she posed as a shepherdess and milkmaid.

Ballet dancers had long evinced an eagerness toward naturalness. After Lully, stage dancing had descended into an expressionless classicism, with action hampered by stiff and elaborate costumes. With the appearance of professional dancers, a new type of dance gradually developed. The dancers Camargo and Sallé had much to do with this.

Camargo was born in Brussels in 1710. She made her Parisian debut in 1726 and achieved such popularity that hats, coiffures and clothing were designated *à la Camargo*. To the horror of many, she ventured to shorten her skirts to give her legs more freedom for dancing and introduced tight-fitting drawers to enable her to leap without endangering her modesty. Although she really represented the old *danse mécanique,* her Spanish ancestry seems to have imparted a new folklike gaiety which enchanted the public.

Marie Sallé, Camargo's contemporary, was born in Paris in 1714. After her first appearance at the Opera when only seven, she became the darling of Paris. In 1734, she was invited to dance in London's Covent Garden and was advised to invent her own dances. With enthusiasm she embarked on a new course and became the first naturalistic dancer of the century, inventing stories and costumes. The London correspondent of the *Mercure de France* reported to Paris, "She dared to appear in this entrée without pannier, skirt or bodice, with her hair down: she did not wear a single ornament on her head. Apart from her corset and petticoat, she wore only a simple dress of muslin draped about her, in the manner of a Greek statue."

Mlle Sallé created an immediate sensation, which was quickly observed by the watchful Handel. Craftily seeking to lure a paying public, he produced two ballet operas for Sallé in 1735, *Ariodante* and *Alcina.* These are filled with all the minutes, gavottes and sarabandes of the day, as well as all kinds of magical props, for Alcina was a sorceress, who transformed her lovers into animals amidst a stage filled with smoke, thunder and lightning.

At first, the French found Sallé too daring for them, but, when the composer Rameau wished to present his second dramatic work in 1735, the ballet-opera, *Les Indes Galantes,* she was invited to

Une Scène d'Opéra, *Rameau's* Indes Gallantes. Courtesy the New York Metropolitan Museum of Art, Harris Brisbane Dick Fund, 1930

appear as the rose in the Persian festival. Thereafter she performed in many of his ballets.

Jean Philippe Rameau, the great French composer of the time, was known chiefly as a composer of pieces for clavecin until he was fifty. These summed up the clavecin technique of French salon composers. Since it was fashionable to write descriptive pieces portraying natural objects in sound, Rameau wrote "Les Oiseux" (The Birds), "La Poule" (The Chicken), and "La Follette," a rondeau. He even attempted to imitate such natural sounds as gusts of wind stirring up whirls of dust in "Les Tourbillons."

Rameau's music was eminently suited to the dance, for he had a natural dramatic instinct and a flare for writing music adaptable to dance mimicry. His tunes had characteristics of shepherds, savages, gentlemen and priests. As he composed, he carefully plotted the dance actions and gave definite directions. Thus, before a sarabande dance by a *zéphyre* and a *nymphe* in his *Zéphyre,* he noted "flutes, with which Zéphyre runs to the nymphe," and so forth.

Yet, in general, Rameau followed the pattern established by Lully. The eighteenth-century ballet was fashioned about the dance forms. Each act had its set dances and each dancer had his and her speciality. Mlle Sallé and M. Dumoulin excelled in graceful musettes; Camargo specialized in the tambourin.

In time Rameau became renowned all over Europe as the great opera composer. He collaborated with Voltaire in 1745. Later he joined forces with Rousseau. This occurred only once! Then Rameau spent his last ten years fighting the great philosopher who regarded himself as a musician and music theorist, even writing a system of musical notation which was rejected by the French Academy. In time the rivalry between the two became a political affray between the king and his mistress, Mme de Pompadour, against the queen, who favored Rousseau and the Encyclopedists. Among these was the philosopher Diderot, who attacked Rameau's operatic ideals and disdained the principle of the magic acts with their elaborate machinery, saying, "The enchanted world may serve to amuse children. The real world alone pleases the mind."

After Rameau, the opera-ballet again degenerated, and the leadership passed from the musician to the choreographer. Here too, a change had long been brewing, for, as early as 1721, John

Weaver, the English translator of Feuillet's *Chorégraphie*, had published an anatomy for dancers. Soon a ballet master appeared, in the person of Noverre, who made such knowledge a prerequisite for his dancers.

Jean Georges Noverre fought to lead the ballet back to naturalism. With his advent the classicism of baroque dancing began to recede. Noverre cried "Nature! Nature!" and advised dancers to forget their legs, feet and arms, to concentrate on gesture and facial expression. He defied tradition and asserted that masks must be disposed of, so must panniers and headdresses, for they hindered the expression of passion. Further, the classical symmetry of dance figures must be dropped since nature did not consider whether one danced four steps to the right and two to the left. Dancing must be natural!

The young Noverre had made his debut in Fontainebleau at sixteen and even acted as ballet master at the Opéra Comique in Paris in 1754. From there he was invited to various cities in Europe. Eventually, the Duke of Wurttemberg called him to Stuttgart, where he penned his novel artistic beliefs. Stuttgart was an artistic center visited by many notables, among whom was the great dancer Vestris, known as the "God of the Dance," and who sired a great dynasty of dancers. Indeed, most great dancers for the ensuing two hundred years could trace their heritage to Vestris. He was so impressed by Noverre that he spread his fame to Vienna, Warsaw, Italy and eventually to Paris.

In 1767, Noverre was summoned to Vienna to superintend the fetes of the marriage of Archduchess Caroline. There, he composed a dozen ballets including *Semiramis* with the music of Gluck. Here also he met the dancer Angiolini who soon became his rival. Angiolini had been trained by the Viennese Hilferding, who was soon called to St. Petersburg, to which city Angiolini himself would soon be called, but not before he collaborated with Gluck in the latter's first great ballet masterpiece, *Don Juan*. Thereafter Gluck collaborated with Noverre.

In 1774, both Gluck and Noverre were summoned to Paris by their pupil Marie Antoinette and the French Academy. The two artists worked in the closest harmony on several productions, including the celebrated *Iphigenia*. Noverre wrote a long paragraph regarding this partnership: ". . . In place of writing steps to written airs, as couplets are set to known melodies, I composed, if I may so express myself, the dialogue of my ballet, and then had music written to fit each phrase and thought. Thus I explained to Gluck the characteristic air of the Ballet of the Savages in *Iphigenia in Tauris:* the steps, gestures, attitudes and expressions of the different characters . . . and gave to this celebrated composer the basis for that fine musical composition."

It is notable that Mozart wrote *Les Petits Riens* to Noverre's scenario in 1778. Noverre's life had a succession of failures, yet his ideas eventually triumphed. Costumes, dances and personages had to conform to the plot of the ballet and the sequence of stereotyped dances was replaced by a flow of action. Yet Noverre held that it was essential to know the five positions which had been established by Beauchamps. Noverre's principles lived on with the great dancers of the future, in Salvatore Vigano, Carlo Blasis, Taglioni, even in Michel Fokine of the twentieth century.

In the field of music, Gluck was almost the last great musician to give direction to the ballet until Stravinsky. And it must be borne in mind that his death in 1787 occurred near the end of the Ancien Regime, rather than at the end of the century. For, although the nineteenth century saw the spectacular development of the romantic ballet, for fifty years hardly a single great score was composed expressly for the dance by a great composer, while, for a hundred and twenty-five years, music did not assume any prominent part in ballet. The choreographers reigned supreme until the twentieth century and Diaghilev. True, Beethoven wrote the score of *The Creatures of Prometheus* (1813) for the great Italian dancer Salvatore Vigano, whose ideals were similar to Noverre. Gretry also composed several melodious ballets; later Adam, Delibes and Tschaikovsky wrote partitions for ballet. However, at this particular time, choreographer was far more important than the composer.

During the Rococo period, as might be expected, many social dances of rustic origin were imported from various countries.

The *loure* was an old French dance from Normandy, resembling the bourrée in measure and movement. Its name came from the old French instrument, the loure, which accompanied it. From the association of this nasal bagpipe with the dance, the term "loure" came to refer to a passage which should be played in the style of a bagpipe air, while the verb *lourer* came to indicate that a performer should play legato with a slight accent on the first note of each group. The *loure* is a short dignified composition in 3/4 time which appears in some eighteenth-century suites.

The *forlane* or *furlana* was an Italian peasant dance from Friuli. Carlo Blasis says it was in vogue with the Venetian gondoliers. In 1895, Lilly Grove Frazer stated that it was performed by two gondoliers who whirled giddily, sometimes imitating rowing or pulling of the oars. It is also called a wild wooing dance, in many respects similar to the tarantella although it is more rugged and irregular. Casanova danced it in 1775 and found no national dance more violent. This seems to be borne out in the forlana in Campra's *Fêtes Vénétiennes* (1710) where the second section is related to have an orgiastic quality.

Forlana dating from seventeenth century (from Schubart's Tanzmusik*)*

The music is in 6/8 time. There seems to have been a typical forlana air using a short haunting minuet motif. Being in rondo form, it may be endlessly repeated. Few examples appear in suites, although Bach included one in his orchestral suite in C. The dance was included in many French operas and Viennese ballets in the seventeenth and eighteenth centuries. Ravel wrote a famous example for piano in the twentieth century.

The *tambourin* was a lively dance from old Provence, originally accompanied by a flute and the long, narrow drum called the *tambour de Basque,* from which the dance is named. When it was adapted to the stage, the drum accompaniment remained a characteristic feature. It is also incorporated into instrumental compositions, where it appears as the repeated single tones in the bass accompaniment.

The music is in 2/4 time. Rameau's well-known tambourin in E minor appears in his suites and he included the dance in his ballets.

The *reel* is a lively gliding dance, probably of Celtic (Scottish

I^ier Tambourin (from Rameau's Dardanus)

or Irish) origin, although its resemblance to a national Danish dance often ascribed a Scandinavian origin to it. It may have been introduced to Great Britain in the time of Alfred the Great. Its figures bear striking resemblances to the rounds and dances of ancient and medieval times. Yet they sometimes reveal the strong influence of the English country dances, which are certainly stylized versions of the primitive round.

The reel is performed on tiptoe by two or more couples who dance in a circular movement. The performers face each other and weave in and out to describe a series of figures of eight. In describing a Scottish reel, Edward Scott relates, in his *Dancing for Strength and Beauty,* that his first disappointment in the dance was magically dispersed when two or three pipers entered to strike up their wild and barbaric music. Invested with this traditional glamour, the dancers formed sets, joined hands and circled about in the characteristic introductory *moulinet,* then went through the reel of eight proper, with each dancer, as "fairy" or "de'il," performing his or her solo as the rest joined hands and circled. This continuous ever-winding movement alternated with the setting to partners and opposite dancers, the turning with the arms and perfect figure eights.

In various countries the reel is performed differently. The slower Highland reel, called the Strathspey after the Scottish district, requires greater exertion than the Scottish reel proper or the Irish reel, which is more rapid, yet with an even musical accompaniment,

Rhythm of "Strathspey" (from Wm. Marshall's "Marchioness of Huntly")

in equal eighth notes. The Strathspey is characterized by the jerky dotted rhythm known as the "Scotch snap." Strangely enough, Scottish reels were never intended for the bagpipes. The first collection of Scottish reels was published by Richard Bremner in 1757.

The Norwegian reel, the *Hälling,* begins slowly, but the dancers gradually quicken their pace to a frenzy; finally, as if the dancers are exhausted, the pace loses speed and concludes as it began.

The *Ecossaise* was another Scottish dance brought to France during the last years of the monarchy. Its name first appeared in 1760, when Voltaire wrote considerably in his letters about an écossaise performed by his sister, Mlle Denis. Yet the écossaise is really a creation of French dancing masters. Furthermore it has little in common with the Scottish dance known as the *Schottisch.*

Ecossaise (Beethoven)

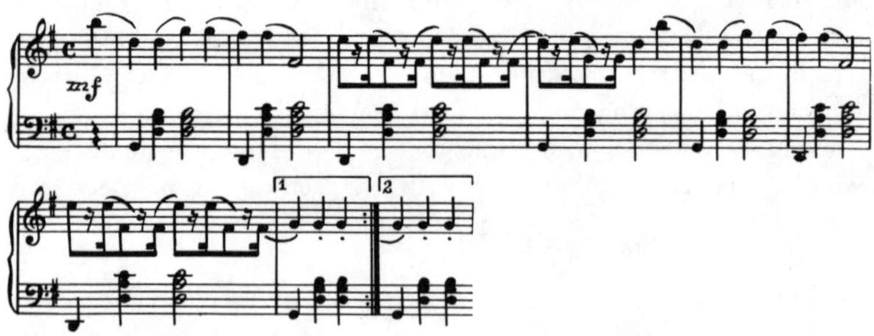

"Les Dentelles de Bruxelles" (a schottische by A. Wallerstein, Opus 79)

Böhm calls the écossaise a turning dance. Czerwinsky relates it to the English country dance (*anglaise*) wherein the men stand next to each other in a long row and the women face them three or four steps apart. The uppermost pair danced in a circle and vigorously swung in a wheelbarrow turn, a triumphant march and other movements, until they breathlessly reached the end of the row.

In Germany the écossaise was first danced as a Scottish round in 1800, and it eventually superseded the older and slower anglaise, which it resembled. It is written in 2/4 or 4/4 meter and was originally accompanied with bagpipes.

Schubert wrote many écossaises for piano; most of Beethoven's were apparently intended for dancing.

The *siciliana* or *sicilienne* was imported from Sicily, where it was anciently a shepherd dance of tender and idyllic nature accompanied by the flute and embellished by the shaking of a tambourine or a handkerchief, even by hand-clapping. The great seventeenth-century Italian composers first adopted the form. Handel followed their example especially for vocal music, as did Mozart, Meyerbeer and others.

The music is rather like a pastoral jig in 6/8

"The Siciliano" (from Scarlotti)

or it may be in 12/8 meter. It is in rondo form and usually in minor.

The *rondo* or *rondeau* is frequently mentioned in association with the dances of the old regime. It has become a purely musical form with no stated dance feature, which relies on the principle of repetitions of a main melody after the introduction of secondary musical ideas. It is a form based on the form originated in the old dance rounds of the ancients and the rondels of the troubadours. Constantly developing from the simple dance with refrain, the rondeau eventually became extended into lengthy orchestral works.

A Ball at the Court of Napoleon, *B. Zix and C. Guerin, Strasbourg, 1810. The line drawing commemorates a celebration for Napoleon and Marie Louise. Note the positions of the arms and the Empire styles. The couples are dancing the allemande.*

15

The Napoleonic Era and the Waltz

As IS CUSTOMARY after wars or political disturbances, dancing became a popular rage after the French Revolution. People satisfied their craving for excitement in a craze for balls, and dance halls opened all over Paris.

The revolution swept away almost all vestiges of the courtly life. Fine manners and fine clothes became dangerous possessions; and tight lacing, as well as paint, powder, wigs and patches went out with the gods and goddesses of courtly life. In 1796, fashions began to imitate the clothing of classical sculpture with high waists, close up to the arm and shorter skirts. Thus began the Empire style, named after the emerging Napoleonic Empire.

Dancing mirrored the novel political and social convictions. The ceremonious graces of the courtly dances were discarded; freer and simpler dances were introduced, many possessing the spirited vulgarity of the lower classes. Although many Europeans still performed the dances of the past, the hops and skips of country dances became preeminent in the ballrooms of France and England. Later, coincident with Napoleon's desire to establish a royal court, the slow and graceful allemande reappeared.

The new *allemande* was quite different from the old dance of the suite. Its music was simpler and devoid of the elaborate figurations of former days; its flowing 3/4 time was rather like the slow waltz which was coming into favor, although some allemandes were slightly quicker.

The greatest charm of the allemande lay in the graceful manner in which the gentleman glided under his lady's arm, and the partners raised and crossed their arms overhead. During their various steps, they never relaxed these pretty attitudes. The dance had three steps, made in a sliding manner backward and forward, and the partners seldom turned around as in the waltz. In our picture of Napoleon at Strasbourg in 1810, the dancers are performing the allemande.

In his capacity as imperial composer, Mozart wrote a number of allemandes, many being intended for the masked balls held at the imperial ballrooms of the Hofburg, where all classes of the population danced minuets, contradances, landlers and the *Deutsche Tanzes,* the latter being allemandes, for the word means German. Even the Emperor, Joseph II (1741-1790), appeared with his suite and mingled in the dancing, although of course the upper classes did not participate in the landler and other German dances.

Von Weber wrote six allemandes for piano (op. 4). Beethoven wrote many, some of which were played as dance music at the Ball of the Society of Plastic Arts, given at the assembly rooms in Vienna on November 22, 1795. It is interesting that Beethoven's allemandes begin on the third beat of the measure, whereas Weber's began on the first.

The most important feature of the era was not the popularity of the allemande, but the rise of its German relative, the *waltz.*

The *waltz* was the democratic successor to the other great dance in triple meter, the aristocratic minuet. The minuet had been the queen among dances when courtiers worshipped at the throne of studied grace and gallant gesture, but the new society found its figures too difficult and too slow. They sought more exhilaration and physical enjoyment from dancing and greeted the close embraces and quicker tempo of the waltz with ardor.

The origin of the waltz has been disputed. The French asserted it descended from the ancient volta, and Germans changed the name to *Valse.* But they overlooked the fact that the old turning dance with the characteristic clasp under the bust was first mentioned and pictured in Germany. The historian Böhm even holds that the origins of the waltz go back to the Minnesingers of the twelfth century and relates it to what is termed the varied-couple dances, in which a slower dance in duple meter is followed by a *Springtanze,* which was a lively dance in triple meter.

Quite correctly, the Germans claim the waltz first appeared as an offspring of their ancient *Drehtanz* and the *Ländler* in 3/8 and 3/4 meter. One proof may be the fact that the famous Viennese conductor and composer Lanner (1801-1840) first called his dances *Ländler* or *Deutscher* up to his opus #7.

The *Ländla* was a true German folk dance for closed couples. Its name came from Landl, a mountain region of Austria sometimes called the Steirer, after Steirermark. Older names for this round dance are *Landerer, Oberländer* (landlers danced in the uplands) and *Schleifer* (slides), referring to the sliding movement of the feet, which is preserved in the waltz. The accompanying melodies flow with the greatest of ease and tenderness as the word *Länderische* has come to mean. In the Alpine lands of Austria, landler tunes were called Tyrolienne and are distinctive for their appendant yodelings, wherein the South German males pass from their normal voice to falsetto in a series of continually breaking intervals of sixths in melodies written in the rhythm 3/4

"Tyrolean Waltz" (from Böhm Geschicte)

Commenda, a great expert on Austrian folk dance, says in his book *Der Ländla* (1923) that practically every minstrel had his own copy of landler tunes which were usually handed down from past generations. The notes were almost undecipherable but the music was performed from memory. Commenda adds that, although the musicians strictly followed the 3/4 rhythm, sometimes they so accented the tunes that they seemed to be in 2/4 time, according to the manner in which the dancers divided their steps.

Landlers have been written by many composers of the period, including Mozart, Schubert and Beethoven. The latter is supposed to have been fond of dancing, although his friend Ries says he never really learned to dance in step.

When dancing the landler, partners often spun in opposite directions with hands clasped high overhead, or the girl whirled, touching the upraised hand of her stamping partner as she glided beneath his arm. Often both turned in close embrace. Hamza, in his study of the landler, mentions a figure in which the men let go their partners, and, standing together in a circle, clapped while the girls walked around outside. Then, each took his partner and resumed dancing.

The *waltz* was first heard of in Bohemia, Austria and Bavaria. From there it migrated throughout the world. As early as 1750, the famous Viennese clown Feliz von Kunz (called "Berardon") wrote many musical comedies containing pieces designated *walzer*. German society adopted the dance sometime in the latter quarter of the century. One of the first times the term appears in art music is the *mouvement de valse* which replaces the customary minuet in a sonatine of Haydn (1766). A year later, the French dancing master Chavanne wrote in his *Principes du menuet* that the waltz had no relation to *"la bonne danse."* In 1784, the French composer Gretry wrote a piece entitled *"Air pour valser."*

At first, dancers did not clasp each other in encircling arms. This posture was introduced after the French Revolution had altered ideals of deportment. Instead, dancers started apart, then later lightly placed their fingertips on each other's waists. Each couple performed a slightly turning waltz motion which had a double movement, rotating on their own axis and also describing a larger circle to return to the original position. The music was in two-bar groups, and required six steps and six beats to complete each little circle: thus 3/4

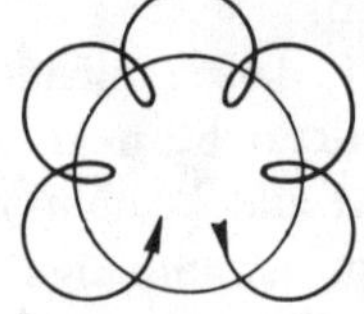

Waltz

1. left foot forward
2. right foot follows
3. turning on left
4. right foot forward
5. left foot follows
6. right turning.

The Waltz, *engraving by J. H. A. Randall (The reference plate to Wilson's* Description of German and French waltzing)

The early waltzes of Mozart, Beethoven and Schubert were usually fairly slow. The Vienna waltz which became the classical form of the dance was noted for its speed, which may have been encouraged by the polishing of floors, for in earlier days floors were rough, and dancers often wore hobnailed shoes and hopped about. The typical rhythm of the Vienna Waltz was 3/4:

3/4 ♩ ♩. ♪ | ♩ ♩. ♪ |

"Vienna Waltz"

After twenty years in France and Germany, the waltz was brought to England, where it created a sensation. Mothers were shocked to see couples familiarly clasping each other. Even the poet Byron wrote a scathing poem on "The Waltz." The furor ebbed after Czar Alexander I of Russia, resplendent in medals, performed it with society leaders in Almack's in 1815. One English writer, Ralkes, related that, although he had once spent mornings lounging in the park, after the introduction of the waltz, he spent them absorbed at home in practicing the figures of a French quadrille, or whirling a chair round the room to learn the step and measure of the German waltz. He adds, "What fear and trembling in the debutantes at the commencement of a waltz, what giddiness and confusion at the end."

Numerous varieties of the waltz appeared during its long life. There was a waltz with a hop, the fast swirling waltz with continual pivoting of couples, which was the favorite. In 1839, Paris was captivated by the Russian two-step waltz (a *deux pas*) with the rhythm 3/4

3/4 ♩ | ♩ 𝄽 ♩ | ♩ 𝄽 ♩ | ♩

Two-step waltz

with a strongly accented first beat. Finally in the twentieth century came the difficult hesitation waltz.

The Romantic composers all favored the waltz. Beethoven's were written for actual dancing; Schubert made the dance into an art form; Chopin made it high art, and von Weber's "Invitation to the Dance" made it into program music.

The form of waltz compositions was set by the Viennese dance composers, Lanner, Labitsky and both the Strausses. This consisted of a slow introduction followed by a series of five or six waltzes in varied rhythms and tempi, concluding with a coda which echoes the best tunes. Most waltzes were given names like "Tales of the Vienna Woods" and the "Blue Danube."

The waltzes of the younger Strauss were so lilting and irresistible that in time their fame became synonymous with the gaiety and beauty of Vienna where he lived and wrote. Strauss's success was due to the charming variety of the rhythm and speed of each little waltz unit, which represented each variety of the dance, the Viennese, the two-step, the hop and others. This gave a good dancer who knew each style an opportunity to vary his step and motion.

The Polka and the Galop

In 1830, the favored dances of Parisian society were the waltz and the galop, the latter being named because the sound of dancers' feet resembled quickly galloping horses.

Galop (from Offenbach's Orphée aux Enfers*)*

The dance originated in Hungary or Germany. Johann Strauss, senior, wrote twenty-four galops.

The galop composed by Offenbach for his opera *Orpheus in Hades* is famous as the accompaniment for the first *cancan,* the famous dance of the Parisian music halls of the gay nineties, wherein the dancers kick off the hats of spectators. The galop from Bizet's piano duets, "Jeux d'Enfants," has been frequently used in movie versions of the cancan.

Cancan

When the eighteen-year-old Victoria was crowned queen of England in 1837, the dance music of Johann Strauss, the elder, brightened the festivities. Victoria is said to have been a graceful dancer, and from 1838 had two rooms in Buckingham Palace set aside for dancing, the throne room and the ballroom. These were connected by a fine gallery. For special occasions, an orchestra played in each. At a royal ball, Her Majesty and the court entered the ballroom before ten o'clock, and she opened the entertainment by choosing her partner for the first quadrille. Later in the evening she progressed to the second room. Waltzes were the favored dance, but the young queen was known to lead a country dance far into the night. After her marriage in 1840, the polka was introduced to the dance program and twenty years later the Lancers was added to state balls.

The gay and vivacious *polka* swept European society to a heat of enthusiasm. It revolutionized dancing and created a dance mania among all classes which few escaped. The polka was a couple dance of Czech origin, and polka tunes have the rustic quality of Czech dances.

One story holds that the dance came into existence when a

Polka

Waltz

dancing teacher, Joseph Neruda, while touring, observed a Czech servant girl singing to herself while improvising a dance. Delighted, he took notes of her performance and brought them to Paris in 1840 and later to London. The dance attained quick fame, creating a furor in Paris and sensations in Vienna and London. The celebrated ballet stars Cerito, Grisi, and Perrot performed the polka at the Paris Opera. Soon clothing, hats, streets were all named after the dance. A dress designer even invented the polka dot.

Dance teachers all claimed they taught the only correct method to perform it. Most of them differed. Although the original polka had ten figures, only five of these were used in the ballroom. All were executed in the polka step. The name was adapted from the Czech *pulka,* meaning "half" or chain step. Originally this was a lively movement in which the feet of both partners flew into the air, and head, trunk, and arms moved vigorously.

The *London News* described one version of the dance with a characteristic heel-and-toe step in which each couple raised first their right legs, then struck the left heels twice with the right heels, then turned as in a waltz. This characteristic step was soon dropped, probably on account of its difficulty, for, as the tabloid *Punch*

La Polka, *colored lithograph by C. Vernier*. Courtesy the New York Public Library

declared, "Dancers usually stamped their heels upon other dancers' toes." Indeed, the *London News* added that its version of the polka was a noiseless dance with no stamping of heels, toes, or kicking legs in sharp angles forward.

The music was played in the slow tempo of a military march with four beats to the bar. Steps were taken during the three beats. The third beat was slightly accented and one foot was drawn sharply behind the other while the toe tip lightly touched the floor.

The phrase was eight bars in length, and the rhythmic figure overlapped into two-bar divisions, with the figure found in the fourth and eighth bars of all early polkas. Originally there was a slight pause in the dance at its appearance, but later this pause was dropped since the tempo of the dance increased. Rhythms for the dance:

2/4
L R L   L R L
2/4
2/4
2/4

Polka rhythms

Humperdinck's polka in his *Hansel and Gretel* is perhaps the most famous.

"Annen-Polka" (from J. Straus, Jr.'s Opus 17)

16

The Romantic Era

In the early nineteenth century, a growing interest in the fantastic affected all the arts. After *Grimm's Fairy Tales* was published in 1813, a host of magic stories followed. In 1821, the German opera *Der Freischutz,* by von Weber, had resounding success in Berlin. This tale of German forests unfolded the legend of the Demon Hunter who offered seven magic bullets to the person who would give up his soul.

Romanticism came to Paris after King Louis Philippe ascended the throne. In 1831, the Paris Opera presented *Robert le Diable,* by Meyerbeer, an opera about Robert, a duke of Normandy who is really the son of the Devil by a mortal mother. The Devil tries to win the youth's soul for Hell. The hit of the production was a ballet designed for the great dancer Marie Taglioni in which the ghosts of faithless nuns rose at midnight from the cemetery of a ruined convent and danced about the young duke. The sensational success of the opera made the fortune of the Paris Opera House.

Thereafter, the stage of the opera was overrun by a host of fairies, nymphs, and medieval characters. Women were the great stars of the ballet. Wearing wings and flying above cemeteries and limpid pools, they far outdistanced the luckless males who pursued them. These were thin, fairylike females who rose to the points of their toes for the first time in history and appeared to defy gravity by the illusion of dainty and airy suspension in midair. This surpassed the elevation achieved by the leaps and kicks of male dancers, who considered toe dancing effeminate, or, what is more likely, were unable to perform *en pointes,* since their bone structure is different from women's.

It is not known who introduced toe dancing. At first it probably consisted of little more than briefly rising to the toe tips. Eventually the reinforced slipper was developed. Admirers of Marie Taglioni feel she may have introduced the points, for they would be most characteristic of her style. Certainly their possibilities must have been apparent to her father, who taught her and planned her choreography from the time of her debut in Vienna in 1821.

Along with toe dancing came gas lighting, with its flickering pools of light enhancing the spectral magic of the Romantic ballet.

With the performance of *La Sylphide* at the Paris Opera on March 12, 1832, Marie Taglioni opened the era of the Romantic ballet. The curtain parted to reveal a Scotch farm lad dreaming of the *sylphide,* an ethereal blue-winged creature who stood before him in a specially designed costume of vaporous white tulle. He wakened as she kissed him; then she vanished up the chimney. The second act commenced in a mysterious glade, where a witch traced a magic circle and conjured up fellow witches; later she cast a fatal spell over a spangled scarf which eventually killed the *sylphide.*

Thunderous success greeted the ballet. It became the rage of all European capitals. The plot became the model for numerous Romantic ballets of supernatural beings. The new style of dancing so enchanted the public that there was a golden age of female dancers, such as Ellsler, Cerito, Grisi, and Grahn. Today this style is known as the classic ballet and even continues the costume of the billowing, bell-shaped gauze skirt, the tight bodice with bared arms and shoulders, the pink tights and the satin slippers designed by Eugene Lami for *La Sylphide.*

The French Opera enjoyed a long period of brilliance, from 1830 to 1838, when all cultural interest centered about it like an imperial court. Everyone went to see the opera and the dance-princesses. The poets Byron, Shelley, and Keats were fascinated by the dreamy, unworldly apparitions and the tragic endings. The ballet was so popular that each opera had to have one dance scene, preferably in the second act, for the box on the first floor left, called the *loge infernale,* was occupied by the influential Jockey Club, and these gentlemen did not appear until the end of the first act, just in time to see the fascinating ladies of the dance, many of whom joined them at supper following the

Marie Taglioni in La Syphilde, *G. Lepaulle*

performance. The German opera composer Richard Wagner suffered by daring to break the customs of the Club when he placed the Venusberg scene of Tannhauser in the first act. When the Jockey Club arrived for the second act and found no ballet, they interrupted the rest of the performance with whistles and hisses and caused the withdrawal of the opera from the repertoire.

Although the composers and the music of Romantic ballets were not important, the ballet had wide influence. By the mid-1830s almost every composer tried his hand at fanciful composition. Berlioz started with a *Symphonie Fantastique;* he had a "Dance of the Sylphs" in his *Damnation of Faust,* Liszt had his *Symphony on Dante's Divine Comedy* with "Inferno" and "Purgatory" movements. He also wrote a "Mephisto Waltz" and similar fantastic works.

The seventeen-year-old Mendelssohn had preceded most Romantics with his music of moonlit fairies in the *Midsummer Night's Dream Overture,* which astounded the world in 1826, but undoubtedly this cultured youth from Berlin had known of the new romanticism of Grimm, von Weber, and Taglioni.

The German composer Schumann wrote idealized dance pieces for the piano. The twelve compositions in his *Papillons* are intended to recreate the fanciful picture of the romance of the ballroom from a novel of Jean Paul Richter. Schumann wrote, "You remember the last scene of Flegeljahr–masks–dance–Walt–Vult–masks–Wine–Vult's dancing–exchange of masks–confessions–indignation –revelation–hurried departure–final scene and the departing brother." Schumann's later "Carnival" and "Davidsbundlertanze" follow a similar plan.

Thus we note how the dance affected musical works in the nineteenth century, just as it was to affect them in the early twentieth century.

17

Nationalism in Romantic Dance

The French Revolution brought many new interests into cultural life, aside from the new personal freedoms and expressions of personal emotions in music and the arts. The awareness of national styles appeared in a growing interest in folk legends and poetry, beginning as early as 1765 in England, when Bishop Percy published a collection of national ballads which he had rescued from the hands of the servant who made fires. Later, John Thomson of Edinburgh engaged such composers as Pleyel, Haydn, and Beethoven to write accompaniments for songs and dance melodies of the British Isles. Shortly after, other nations lowered their gaze from the distant aristocratic courts and discovered their own people.

Thus, with the appearance of Romanticism, composers again turned to the inexhaustible spring of the folk dance and introduced a host of new national dance forms. And, after 1830, society began to dance the Polish mazurka and the schottische, while Chopin, Liszt, and other composers introduced the rhythms of Poland, Hungary, and Czechoslovakia.

Nationalism was identified on the stage with the dancer Fanny Ellsler, a young Viennese, whose fame reached that of her contemporary, Taglioni, although her earthly energy was the opposite of feminine fragility. Gautier reported, "Fanny is a very pagan dancer, she recalls the muse, Terpsichore, tambourine in hand, her tunic exposing her thigh, caught up with a gold clasp. When she bends freely from her hips, throwing back her swooning voluptuous arms, we visualize one of those beautiful figures from Herculaneum or Pompeii which stand out in white relief against a black background, intensifying their steps with resounding cymbals."

Ellsler excelled in fiery character dancing, in folk dances in which she satisfied the Romantic appetite for the exoticism of strange lands: the tarantella from Italy, the cracovienne from Poland. In Spain she found the graceful *cachucha* with its Bolerolike rhythm in seeming contradiction of its 3/8 meter.

Ellsler's first performance of the cachucha in the ballet *Le Diable Boiteux* (1836) so amazed Paris that the writer Charles de Boigne observed,

> A certain number of performances were needed to accustom the public to the cachucha. Those swaying hips . . . those provocative gestures, those arms which seemed to seek out and embrace an absent being, that mouth which asked to be kissed, the body that thrilled, shuddered and twisted, that seductive music, those castanets, that unfamiliar costume, that short skirt, that half-open bodice, all this, and especially, Ellsler's sensuous grace, wanton abandon and plastic beauty were greatly appreciated by the opera-glasses of the stalls and boxes. However, the public, the real public, found it difficult to accept such choreographic audacities.

Thus Ellsler, with her fire and naturalism, introduced elements of nationalism and authenticity to the dance. However, her dances were not entirely authentic representations of national dances but her own adaptations according to her academic training.

By the end of the nineteenth century, national feeling became rampant with composers throughout Europe. In Bohemia, Smetana and, later, Dvorak produced a great array of Czech works; Grieg included the dance rhythms of his native Norway in his "Norwegian Dances" arranged for piano and the "Symphonic Dances." Later the Russians entered the field. A strange fact was the Romantic exploitation of Spanish dances and dance rhythms by composers of other lands before the appearance of Albeniz, Granados, and De Falla.

In utilizing national dances, the Romantic composers did more than use their rhythm and form, but made them the vehicle for the utterance of their own feelings and as the expression of their fantasies. Thus their dances often embodied the three characteristics of the era: the desire to express individuality, the love of the fantastic, and nationalism.

Liszt felt that Chopin should be ranked among the first musicians to individualize themselves in the poetic sense of an entire nation, not only because he adopted the rhythm of polonaises, mazurkas and the cracoviennes, and called his works by their names, but also because he filled these forms with feelings typical of his country. Perhaps Chopin's polonaises illustrate this statement to its full extent.

The Polonaise

The *polonaise* is said to have originated in the courtly festivities of Poland during the late sixteenth century. Although it is often considered a dance, it was really the music used to accompany a sort of procession. A popular legend related that one year after Henry III of Anjou, son of Catherine de Medici, was elected king of Poland in 1573, he held a great reception at Cracow, Poland, wherein the nobility and their wives, arrayed in their most dazzling gowns and most magnificent uniforms, marched in procession before the throne to the sound of stately music. From this, the custom developed of opening court festivities with marchlike music called *polonaise*. And, thereafter, whenever a foreign prince was elected to the Polish throne, the same ceremony was repeated. However, neither the name nor the type of music appears among Polish dance melodies, and even the Polish name, *Polonez* may have come from the French, for the polonaise was not mentioned until a French writer praised it in 1645.

Eventually Polish nobles began to perform a polonaise in their homes and palaces upon especially festive occasions. This took the form of a circling promenade led by the master of the house, who conducted the procession of his guests, who were expected to follow every action of their leader. Liszt describes such a polonaise in his *Life of Chopin,* relating how the entire group slowly glided like swans over the water, moving with a rhythmic, cadenced, and undulating step. Sometimes the gentleman offered his right, sometimes his left hand to his partner; sometimes he passed to her right or to her left, touching only the points of her fingers, or clasping her slight hand within his own. These complicated movements were instantaneously imitated by every pair and ran like an electric shiver through the entire length of this gigantic serpent.

The music of the early polonaises possesses more historical than artistic value. Many do not bear the names of their composers but are marked by the name of a contemporary hero, such as "Kosciuszko." During the seventeenth century, the music assumed its present form, but it was not until the eighteenth century that polonaises of artistic value began to appear. The form achieved sudden popularity in Germany undoubtedly due to the election of Augustus III of Saxony to be king of Poland. Augustus III also seems to have been instrumental in introducing the Polish mazurka into Germany. Thereafter the polonaise became a favorite form for instrumental composers.

J. S. Bach wrote many polonaises, including the polacca in the "Brandenburg Concertos" (#I Dehn), the magnificent polonaise in the orchestral "Partita in B minor" and that in the "French Suite in E." Handel wrote a polonaise; Mozart wrote a rondeau polonaise in his triple concerto, which he dedicated to the empress of Russia in 1815. Schubert wrote polonaises for four hands, and von Weber composed a Polacca Brillianté Opus 72 as well as Opus 21.

The *polacca* can be briefly described as a polonaise written in a more brilliant or Italian manner. Although polaccas have more ornaments than polonaises, nevertheless they retain much of the characteristic Polish rhythm.

Liszt asserted that von Weber restored the pristine and vanished magnificence to the polonaise. However the form reached a high state of development through the genius of Chopin, for he was so attracted by the striking rhythmic possibilities and national vigor, that he reanimated the old form and changed it into a tone picture which proclaimed the glory, the griefs, and the hopes of the Polish people.

The distinctive rhythm of the polonaise is characterized by a strong emphasis on the second beat of the bar.

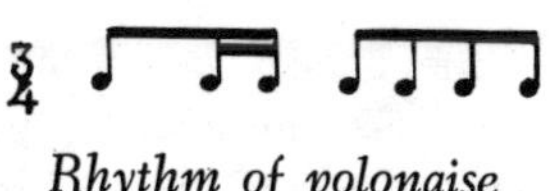

Rhythm of polonaise

Often there is a trill of eighth notes on the first beat. The concluding cadence ends on the third beat of the measure:

Typical ending of a polonaise

in a fashion typical of sixteenth-century Polish dances.

The distinctive rhythm seems to have been a later development, for the dance did not lose the duple rhythm of a slow gliding introductory dance until the beginning of the eighteenth century. Possibly the change from duple to triple meter sprang from the same baroque tendency which caused triple meter to be preferred for dancing, and made the sarabande and minuet favored above the branle, basse danse and pavane. We note that the rhythmic figure

had been a dance feature for centuries. Arbeau says it was the drum accompaniment of the pavane, while such dances as the fourteenth-century saltarello and its successor, the galliard, and certainly the *lamento di tristano* possessed a rhythm similar to the polonaise of Chopin's day.

The Mazurka

Nineteenth-century composers have perpetuated European national dance forms such as the tarantella, tango, the sequidillas and the polonaise. Among these is the *mazurka,* which derived its name from the women of the Polish duchy of Mazovia, who were called *Mazurkas.*

In Bach's lifetime, the dance was introduced to Germany by Augustus III, the elector of Saxony who was elected king of Poland. By 1840, the mazurka was danced all over Europe, being extremely fashionable in Paris during the time of Chopin, whose fondness for the form has perpetuated it. Yet his mazurkas often have a most original treatment. True, he used Polish melodies, but these were refined and the form extended. Actually his mazurkas are idealized, and imaginative dances of a tone poet, stamped by the personality and whims of the composer.

Originally, this was the only choral circle dance for an unlimited number of dancers. In the sixteenth century, it was a rustic dance and six to eight couples danced to a song. The form had either two or four parts of eight bars; each was repeated. Never are there three parts or more than four. A round or circle was danced in the first part; in the second part the first dancers circled about; then the others imitated them by turns. The feet were stamped in characteristic fashion; also the heels were struck together once the first time round, twice the second time, and thrice the third time.

The music suits the steps and actions of the dancers, being very free and capricious in accent and rhythm. Certain parts almost seem to be in two-beat measure. This rhythmic changeability once caused a heated argument between Chopin and Meyerbeer, who entered a room while Chopin was playing his "Mazurka in C," opus 33 #3. Meyerbeer remarked that the piece was in 2/4; Chopin insisted it was in 3/4. In the argument, the conductor, Charles Hallé, sided with Meyerbeer, but Chopin laughingly observed this rhythmic vagary was a national characteristic of the dance.

Mazurka (from Chopin's Opus 33, #3)

The peculiarities of the mazurka include:

1. The first beat of the bar is often broken.
2. The second beat is frequently accented.
3. The third beat is often emphatic.
4. The complete metrical measure always consists of two bars (six beats).

5. Each period contains eight measures.
6. The tune ends on the second beat, so that the third beat often belongs to the next phrase.
7. In addition, the bass of early mazurkas usually consisted of a tonic pedal-point.

In his *Life of Chopin* (translation of J. Broadhouse, London, 1913), Liszt writes that only in Poland could one observe

> the haughty, yet tender and alluring character of this dance. The cavalier, always chosen by the lady, seizes her as a conquest of which he is proud, striving to exhibit her loveliness to the admiration of his rivals, before he whirls her off in an entrancing and ardent embrace. . . . After the Mazurka commenced, the attention, in place of being distracted by a multitude of people jostling against each other without grace or order, is fascinated by one couple of equal beauty, darting forward, like twin stars, in free and unimpeded space. As if in the pride of defiance, the cavalier accentuates his steps, quits his partner for a moment, as if to contemplate her with renewed delight, rejoins her with passionate eagerness, or whirls himself rapidly round, as though overcome with sudden joy and yielding to the delicious giddiness of rapture. Sometimes two couples start at the same moment, after which a change of partners may occur between them, or a third cavalier may present himself and, clapping his hands, claim one of the ladies as his partner. The queens of the festival are in turn claimed by the most brilliant gentleman present, courting the honor of leading them through the dance.

Liszt further commented that, although in Chopin's mazurkas we sometimes catch the sounds of the rattling of spurs, it is often "the almost imperceptible rustling of crepe and gauze under the light breath of the dancers. . . . Again, in some, the rhythm is as floating, as undetermined as . . . the feelings of two young lovers."

In the mid-nineteenth century, several offspring of the mazurka appeared, one being the polka-mazurka, a mixed species in 3/4, in which a mazurka step was joined to the polka; the feet never entirely left the floor; and great use was made of the knees which bent and straightened continuously. Johann Strauss, the younger, wrote several examples of this dance.

Nineteenth Century National Dances

The *tarantella* is Italy's most famous national dance. It was highly favored by the Romantic composers. It derived its name from Taranto, in the old province of Apulia, in southern Italy.

The tarantella acquired a fictitious fame from the belief that a strange type of insanity from the bite of the Lycosa Tarantula, the largest of European spiders, could be cured only by dancing to exhaustion. *Grove's Dictionary* informs us that a disease known as Tarantism existed in southern Italy in the fifteenth, sixteenth and seventeenth centuries. Apparently this disease created a sort of hysteria, similar to the earlier St. Vitus's dance epidemic in Germany. The tale of the bite of the spider is quite improbable since the bite of a tarantula is no more poisonous than the sting of a wasp.

The Tarantism story seems more like the stories of medieval dance manias where people were cursed to dance in churches and graveyards. Indeed, the first notice occurs in Niccolo Perotto's *Cornucopia Linguae Latinae* in 1489. When the epidemic was at its height in the sixteenth century, musicians apparently traversed the country to play the music which was the only healing medicine. Different forms of the disease were supposedly cured by different airs, to which the sufferers danced until they dropped from exhaustion. Most of these songs have vanished, although the Jesuit father Athanasius Kircher preserved a few which are not in Mendel's Lexicon. These are written in common time and in the ecclesiastical modes and have no resemblance to the modern dance, which is in rapid 6/8 time.

Tarantella (from Mendelssohn's "Song without Words," Opus 102, #3)

In performance, the Italian tarantella has little relationship to the dance madness. Curt Sachs relates it to the Roman *saltarello* and the Tuscan *tresca*. This is a natural rustic dance of the Italians, a race noted for spontaneity in action and their quick flash of eye and impetuous gesture. It is performed by a man and woman, although two or three women may dance it together while playing tambourines and the large-sized Neapolitan castanets. In another description, the gaily dressed dancers timidly saluted and began to dance. First they withdrew as the male gamboled and capered, and again held aloof. Finally he grasped his partner's hands, and they giddily whirled with quick acrobatic turns until the girl collapsed, while her apparently grief-stricken partner sadly regarded her. The musical accompaniment was quick and bold, alternating between major and minor.

Hungarian Music and the Gypsies

Music is indebted to the gypsies who wandered all over Europe from the Russian steppes to Spain, France, and England, bringing the music of one race to another. Originally, gypsies seem to have come from India, being first mentioned there in the eleventh century, certainly words in their language are of *Sanskrit* origin.

For centuries, gypsies have been renowned as wandering musicians and also as soothsayers and mediums for their gift of prophecy. When they gathered together before the flickering campfire, the musicians were expected to entertain with their fiddles and the cembalo—to tell stories with descriptive song and dance. Often these involved a sort of magical rite, to bring good luck to the tribe with the invocation of the devil. Later all joined in the dance, slowly at first, then going faster and faster, until perspiration poured down their faces.

There is no special gypsy music. Tunes were borrowed from the lands the people visited. But the gypsy style of playing these tunes is distinctive, stamped by the personality of the performers and their distant Oriental heredity. Improvisation is the core of this music; the performer slides from note to note, touching the extremities of each interval, exaggerating softness, followed by startling tonal contrasts. Similarly gypsy dancing is free and improvisational.

Hungary seems to have been a fertile soil for the gypsy musician. Yet in spite of the relationship, Hungarian music is not gypsy music but Magyar. When seeking the origin of Hungarian folksongs, the composers Bela Bartok and Zoltan Kodaly found traces of neighboring races—of Slavs, Germans and Italians. We also note echoes of the distant Oriental modes when we hear the arrangements of Hungarian folksongs made by Bartok and Kodaly. We hear the clash of primitive harmonies, and, in the so-called Hungarian minor scale, we note the augumented seconds. The peculiar

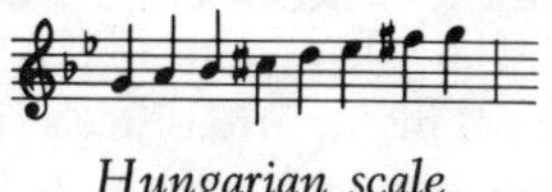

Hungarian scale

embellishments have made notation difficult, and we find such syncopated rhythms as

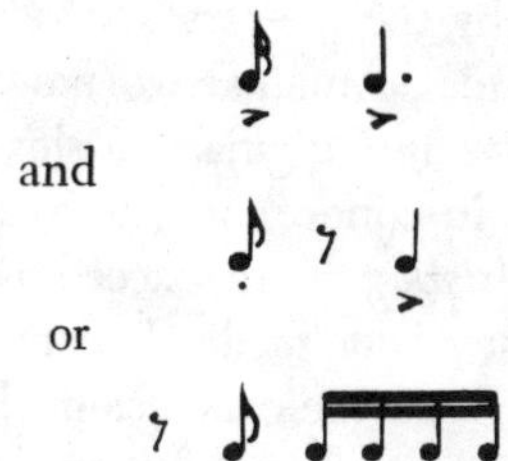

Rhythms of Hungarian dances

in Liszt's "Rhapsody No. 12." In addition there are sudden and unexpected changes in speed.

Despite the popularity of Hungarian music, we find surprisingly few well-known Hungarian dances, possibly because Hungarian music is so improvisational that the dance itself takes on the aspect of free fantasia. In the Hungarian couple dance, the man leads his partner in a slow introduction, then releases her for a lively wooing leap dance. Eventually he takes her hand to repeat the slow introductory section.

The most familiar dance is the *czardas,* a name derived from the Hungarian *tcharda,* meaning tavern or innkeeper. This was a dance of the Hungarian country people and gypsies, originally derived from the Magyar Kor in the nineteenth century. It even may have come from primitive marriage ceremonies. Eventually it became the national dance of Hungary.

The czardas is a dance for couples and presents a lively, colorful, and complex appearance, since none of the couples ever dances the same figures at the same time. There are rapid changes of mood. The figures vary in different districts and no two couples ever dance alike. The czardas typically begins with a stately promenade, which, upon a motion of the dancers to the musicians, changes into a rapid whirling motion. Then the dancers separate and carry on a sort of pantomime wherein the girl alternately approaches and retreats from her partner, who claps his spurred heels together and stamps upon the ground with toe and heel until he finally overtakes and seizes her, whereupon both dancers whirl madly. The pantomime and whirling continue indefinitely. The dancers perform with a proud and lofty air. There is no measured step or movement; everything is improvised by the dancers.

The music of the czardas contains two movements: the first is a slow, songlike *lassu* or *lassan* (originally a slow dance for men in a circle). This is generally in minor in 4/4 or 2/4 meter. The second part, called the *friss* or *friszka,* is an exceedingly lively dance in the same meter but in the major mode. It contains repeated eight-bar to sixteen-bar phrases. Near the conclusion, the tempo is speeded and the music becomes wild and tumultuous.

The fire and precision of Hungarian musicians had placed them in great demand from as early as the thirteenth century, and Hungarian music was used by many great composers. The influence is traceable in Bach, Haydn, and Schubert, although it has been translated into classical terms. Haydn's "Gypsy Rondo," from his "Trio No. 1 in G," is a familiar example, but there are other indications that Haydn conducted the almost entirely Hungarian band of Prince Esterhazy.

By the middle of the nineteenth century, the Hungarian idiom was adopted by such Romantic composers as von Weber, Dvorak, and certainly Brahms, whose Hungarian dances for piano are adaptations of the wild performances of Hungarian bands.

Franz Liszt also echoes the influence of the indigenous bands he heard in his native Hungary. We hear it in his syncopated rhythms in the crashing chords and the sturdy bass accompaniment. Liszt was so fascinated by the gypsies that he wrote a history of

The Gypsy in Music in two volumes. In his twenty "Hungarian Rhapsodies," he reflects as much of the gypsy as the Hungarian. We feel the outpouring of gypsy passion, note the characteristic change of mood from gloom to frenzied abandon. In addition we note how Liszt adopted the curious gypsy ornamentation and echoed the strumming of the cembalo in the accompaniments.

18

The Influence of Spain

THE COLOR AND EXCITEMENT of Spanish music and dancing has been influential for generations. In the sixteenth century, Spain had become a symbol of the exotic and romantic, not only because of her relationship to the Moors, but also because of her adventures in the New World and the riches and gold these brought.

Spanish folk dances are among the richest in racial individuality. With their medieval mystery and seductive plastic forms, as well as their passion, fury, and angelic grace, they form an impressive example of folk art.

The Phoenicians were the first important conquerors of Spain and they left a tradition which still persists. From them came the castanets of the dancing girls and the Phoenician headdress. In ancient Rome, Pliny praised the art and beauty of Spanish dancers at the Roman banquets. The centuries of Inquisition, the romantic tragedies of the Moors, and the harems and silhouettes of the Alhambra are all incorporated. From Africa and Arabia came sensual movements of hip and body. From Central America came the *sarabande* and *chaconne,* later the *fandango, malaguena,* and, more recently, the *habanera* and *tango.* To this exotic blend was added the polish and culture of old Spain, plus the sparkle of the castanets mingling 3/8 and 3/4:

Rhythm of castanets in Spanish music

With the decline of Spain and its trend toward religious restraint, Spanish dances became less popular. However in the nineteenth century a new wave of interest in Spanish culture arose, and we find many new dances, although many of these were imported from Spain's South American cousins.

The fandango is one of the most sensual of courting dances. It is performed by only one couple who continually challenge each other without ever touching. Writing in Madrid in 1767, Casanova noted that no couple moved more than three steps as they clicked their castanets to the music and with a thousand attitudes and gestures they expressed love from the sigh of desire to its culmination.

"El Fandango de Candil" (from Granados)

The *fandango* reputedly came from the American Indians and was well known in eighteenth-century Europe. Gluck supposedly used a genuine folk-dance tune for the fandango in his ballet, *Don Juan,* and this was borrowed by Mozart for the ballet in his opera *Figaro.* One of the best known fandangos is the "Fandango de Candil," found in Granados' *Goyescas.*

The music of the fandango is in 3/4 or 3/8. It accelerates as the dance progresses. Dance and music are noted for sudden pauses, and at certain times the dancing stops while the performers sing.

Many varieties of the fandango bear the names of the city of their origin; the *rondeno* came from Ronda in Andalusia; the *granadina* came from Granada; the *malaguena* originated in Malaga.

Perhaps the malaguena is the most familiar; the best-known composition is that by the Cuban Lecuona. The dance has some more or less improvised singing to poetry in the same style and meter as a *jota.* Written in minor, the harmony of the cadences is particularly notable, for, beginning on the eighth scale step, the bass follows the descending melodic minor scale with a flatted seventh step down to the fifth step, where it concludes. Meanwhile, the upper voices move in parallel thirds, fifths, and octaves.

In the nineteenth century, the fandango was superseded by the *sevillana, bolero,* and the *jota* of Northern Spain.

The jota, called *xota* in old Spanish, stems back as far as the Moors, although Spaniards often claim it descended from the old

"Jota Aragonesa" (from Flores de Espana*)*

canaries. The jota of Aragon is reputedly the most exotic. After centuries of contact with various civilizations, it bears traits of Arabs, Africans, French, Italians, and, of course, the Spanish gypsies.

The *jota* is performed by one or more couples who sing as they dance. The verse structures of the song are supposedly derived from the *coplas* of the Moors. A charming tale relates that the dance was named after a Valencian Moor, Aben-Jot, or Alvenjaldun, a poet and musician who lived in about 1169. The story asserts that the poet had offended the Moslems by inventing a new type of verse form, for Mohammedans were bound by their religious scriptures, the Koran, to avoid new art forms. Aben-Jot was obliged to flee far to Christian Aragon. From this migration, the Aragonese jota differs greatly from that of Catalonia. Thus the second line of the Valencian jota repeats the first line, whereas in Aragon the line is repeated once more at the end, so that it is heard three times.

There are three subjects for the Aragonese jota: those dedicated to the Virgin of Pilar, the patron saint of Aragon; pride in the province of Aragon; and humorous verses about the beloved jota and the beloved Virgin.

The dance accompaniment by guitars, assisted by castanets, has unusual harmonic characteristics. It begins with a showy prelude, which is followed by the song, and is concluded with a showy postlude. The music is noted for the elaborate rhythmic undercurrent of the percussive instruments, wherein the castanets are so hung that they produce a characteristic jota sound, a sort of dry *tak* or *tok*.

Composers using the jota form include Liszt, Glinka, Saint-Saens, and Balakire, as well as such Spaniards as De Falla and Albeniz.

The slow Cuban *habanera* was imported from Havana. The dance is well known because of Bizet's example in *Carmen*. However, Bizet did not compose this music. Instead, when advised that his opera needed a sensuous song, he borrowed Yradier's "Chanson

Havanaise." To Bizet's credit, he always ascribed its origin to Yradier.

"El Areglito" (from S. Yradier's "Chanson Habanaise")

Debussy used this form in his piano compositions "La soirée dans Grenade" and "La puerto del vino." Ravel also wrote "Pièce en forme de habanera."

Other famous South American dances with a Spanish flair include the *tango,* the *rumba,* and the *samba.*

Before concluding our study of Spanish dances, we must include the *bolero,* which is especially famous because of Ravel's great orchestral composition.

The bolero was supposedly discovered by the dancer Zerezo in 1780. Although there are one or two sharply marked rhythmic figures associated with the music, later examples incorporate the rhythm of the castanets to give this figure 3/4 meter.

Bolero rhythm

The dance commences after the introductory clatter of the castanets with a brilliant gravity-defying leap by the man, who, in descending, kicks one foot backward to give his body a half-turn while in the air. Meanwhile, his partner repeats the movement but more daintily; she also raises her arm in the air. Then, with eyes and features, the dance proper commences with long seductive steps, graceful motions of the body and gay upward flings of the arms. In the second part, the dancers execute solos revealing their most sensational and virile motions. Thus the man may include a series of vigorous jumps, executed straight up as he spreads his legs out to horizontal.

The music of the bolero is usually composed in five parts and follows the general pattern of the dance. In the brilliant conclusion, the performers execute gracefully distinguished poses.

The Flamenco Dance

Today, Spain is the land of the gypsy dancer, with *flamenco* dancing accompanied by guitar, castanet, and tambourine.

Each city has its own magic and charm, all bearing the imprint of the long conquest of the land by the Arabs, in Moorish arch and Arabic inscription.

The flamenco is best performed by gypsies who train their most talented children for this, a main source of their livelihood. The female dancers wear dresses with tiers of ruffles; frequently these are long, even with trains. The men wear tight trousers, often topped by a scarf about the waist and a short vest or jacket over a ruffled blouse. The hands and arms play a large part in these dances, and, even when accompanied by castanets, all seem to move with Oriental gestures.

To a large part, these dances are improvised and are set by the mood of the performer. Many start with hand-clapping, until the musicians are ready to commence. A male singer, unaccompanied, intones long wordless Oriental cadenzas, somewhat like those of a cantor in a synagogue. Then we have the strumming of guitars and the typical Spanish tap dance, which must have developed through centuries of performance and is performed with or without accompaniment.

The typical song and dance of Seville is the *sevillana,* performed by couples. With arms calmly twisting to the clacking of castanets in three-beat rhythm, the dancers execute these airy, gracious dances. Meanwhile, the audience claps hands as a singer intones a poetic song to the strumming of the ever-present guitar.

The sevillana is a *seguidilla,* an eighteenth-century Spanish dance, which is the archetype of many dances of Spain.

We here understand the distinctive rhythms, the imitative throbbing of the guitars and clacking of castanets in works of de Falla, Granadas, and Turina. We remember the long tuneful runs, so like the cadenzas of the deep song of the gypsies, and we recall all those dances which are based on the repertoire of the flamenco dancers, the sevillanas, malaguenas, boleros and fandangos.

19

Nineteenth-Century Russian Dancing

BEFORE ENTERING THE TWENTIETH CENTURY, we should discuss Russian dancing.

The westernization of Russian dancing seems to go back to Peter the Great (1672-1725), who introduced the European court dancing of the courante, minuet and pavane which he saw in the West. He commanded wives to accompany their husbands to court, and, if they demurred, guardsmen dragged them to the balls.

Catherine the Great imported Hilferding, Angiolini and later Noverre's pupil, Le Picq, to produce ballets. But the arrival of Marius Petipa to St. Petersburg in 1847 marked the cornerstone of the great Russian School. Petipa was in command for over a half-century, and it was his directives which called upon the great Russian composers of the late nineteenth century, Tschaikovsky, Glinka, Borodin, Drigo, and Glazounov. However, they did not influence the ballet. The ballet master was the dictator.

At this time, the production of a ballet was a hodgepodge. The scenario writer knew little about music or choreography. He planned the story in scenes and acts, based on the principal characters who were the ballerinas, the *premier danseur*, and the *corps de ballet*; their performances had a fixed series of dances to illustrate their abilities. Finally the composer was summoned to write music in the styles of march, polka, galop, waltz, and so forth. He was told how many measures to write and advised about the style of instruments; thus, castanets were Spanish, drums and trumpets were for marches, and so forth.

For the most part, Petipa used the services of hack musicians.

Russischer Bauerntanz, *Ilja Jefimowitsch Rjepin. In this Russian picture, the male dancer appears to be dancing the gopak.*

However a new era commenced in 1875, when Tschaikovsky was commissioned to write *Swan Lake.* Tschaikovsky made careful study of the body and realized that dance music did not require sustained climaxes and clever counterpoint. As a result his dance music is a joy to dancers. Yet, at first, *Swan Lake* had slight success due to difficulties in the production. But, after Tschaikovsky's death in 1893, Petipa became enchanted by the music and revived it with the greatest success. New productions of the *Sleeping Beauty,* Tschaikovsky's favorite, and the *Nutcracker,* were also received with enthusiasm, which has been repeated at every performance ever since.

Nineteenth-century national dances would be incomplete without mentioning the Russian *Gopak* or *Hopak,* which means a two-step, while *Trepak* indicates a three-step. This dance introduces one of the characteristic movements of Russian dances, wherein the male squats in a deep kneebend and, balancing his body on the toes of first one foot, then the other, alternately kicks his feet straight out in front of him in rapid succession, meanwhile keeping the upper part of his body almost stationary. The step is not difficult if the performer is limber; however, in order to achieve a successful performance, the dancer must lean well over to the side of the leg which is about to support the body. At times dancers bring their limbs around with a peculiar action which makes their movements even more grotesque. Sometimes they rapidly progress forward across the floor as they alternately double up and extend their limbs. This motion is not performed by women, who merely sway or slowly circle about as their male partners gyrate.

This squat-flung dance motion is also performed in Spain as the *charrada.* Carvings show that the Etruscans also used it, and the Greeks originally took it from the Persians as the *oklasma.*

A characteristic hopak of the Russian peasants was written by Mussorgski for his opera, *The Fair of Sorotchinski,* in the characteristic 2/4 rhythm.

A Ball at the Tuileries: The Imperial Quadrille, *from* Le Monde Illustré. *Napoleon III with Eugénie. Observe the elaborate skirts worn by the ladies.* Courtesy the New York Public Library

20

Social Dancing after 1850

THE GREATEST EUROPEAN EVENT after 1850 was the creation of the brilliant court of the Second Empire by Napoleon III, in 1852, and its fall in the Franco-Prussian War in 1870.

The establishment of the Court of Napoleon III and his bride, the beautiful Spanish Countess Eugénie, created a new positive dictation of fashion, yet no new dance forms were introduced after 1850, and none was used as the basis of an important musical form. For years the most popular dances in private ballrooms were the waltz and the quadrille. True, the *varsovienne* had a brief popularity, but it was actually a variety of the mazurka in slow 3/4 time.

The *quadrille* was no newcomer; it was a relative of the English country dances, the American square dance, and more anciently, the branle. It was no more than a *contra danse* for four couples in a square. Both Mozart and Beethoven knew it and even wrote minor examples. However, the quadrille achieved a new success in Vienna in 1840 when it was introduced by Johann Strauss the elder, who had learned it in Paris.

In discussing the quadrille of the Second Empire, Vuillier wrote, "There were a considerable number of contredanses, for at this period every dancing master arranged new ones for himself. Every little event served as a pretext for a new arrangement. But the invention of the *Imperial Quadrille* in 1859, by the ephemeral academic society of dancing masters in Paris, was the final creation. The fire of inspiration has since died out."

This dance has no distinctive rhythmic scheme or set melody; it was adapted to known melodies.

The *cotillion* or *cotillon* is a related dance which was developed from the English round for eight, but so transformed, that it was called a *contredanse française.* In turn, this was given the French name *cotillon* ("petticoat") from the popular song:

Ma commère quand je danse	My godmother, when I dance
Mon cotillon va-t-il bien?	Does my petticoat look nice?

Under this name, the dance returned to England as the cotillion.

To perform the dance, four couples arranged themselves in a square, with two men facing their partners on each side. They saluted in the first entrée and executed a figure in the second musical period, returning to the original spot. In another figure they performed a *grande chaine* where dancers joined hands, ladies turned left, and gentlemen turned right, all winding in a circle.

A further variation of these dances appeared as the *quadrille à la cour,* which became called *the lanciers.* It was related that the Parisian dance master Laborde invented the dance in 1856, and it was introduced the following year by the Prussian Court Ballet, wearing lancer uniforms. Actually, the lanciers was danced in Dublin in 1817, and the dance teacher Hart describes its performance in a book published in 1820, *Les Lanciers, a Second Set of Quadrilles for the Piano Forte.*

"Les Lanciers" (a quadrille by Schubert)

The great leader of orchestral dance music during the eighteen years of the Empire was the unsurpassable Johann Strauss the younger, who made Paris the center of his activities. In 1873, when an old man, he came to England to follow the Emperor's coffin to the grave. Parisis, the writer, related a touching circumstance which occurred at that time:

> I remember a pathetic incident at the official reception after the funeral. When the Empress caught sight of the old impresario, the brilliant spectacle of all the past fetes at which she had presided

suddenly rose before her. She clasped her hands together piteously, her eyes filled with tears, and sobs rose in her throat. Strauss said to me as we retired, "I am not like an ordinary person to the Empress, my life and hers have been intimately connected, and from her earliest years my name has been associated with all her happiest memories. I called the first Polka I ever composed, the Eugénie Polka, and dedicated it to the Mademoiselle de Montijo in 1846. The Polka was in its infancy as it were, and was not then danced in official drawing rooms; it was first introduced to the Spanish Court by the 'future' Empress, where she danced it with M. de Courpon, the son of a rich stockbroker, and a famous Cotillon-leader at the Tuileries. Later I saw her in Paris, first in that aristocratic drawing-room where everything artistic was welcomed with so much hospitality, then in that gorgeous salon, where the woman took precedence of the sovereign, and where her irresistible grace and charm tempered the stiffness of court ceremonial. Is it not natural that on seeing me again, the contrast between those happy days and her present situation should call forth an outburst of grief?"

With the defeat of the Second Empire, Europe seems to have become overshadowed by a dark cloud. French influence waned, and Paris temporarily lost her brilliant social life. In England, also, dancing generally followed the same paths of development as that of the continent, and during the latter part of the century, when the black-garbed Victoria lamented her beloved Albert, the art became almost decadent; few dances were introduced and older ones fell into disfavor.

21

The Twentieth Century

The Social Dance

Music and the dance underwent great changes in the first years of the twentieth century as the pace of life steadily quickened. In reaction to sober Victorian formality, youth began to take the place of age. The telephone, radio, and, finally, the airplane linked far-off places. The war brought a taste for distant lands and hastened interest in novel means of expression.

Dancing in statelier days. Cotillion given on January 4, 1901, in the Fifth Avenue home of W. C. Whitney, from a drawing by A. I. Keller for Harper's Weekly

Ragtime dancing in the new ballroom of the Ritz-Carlton Hotel, New York. The society craze for dancing strange new steps spread over the country. (Section of a drawing by F. Matania for the London Spur, 1913*)*

Old customs weakened, clothing changed, skirts became shorter. Composers like Scriabin and Debussy brought new musical idioms. The world swept into the jazz age.

Whereas, earlier, Americans, influenced by Puritan restraints, had often frowned on the dance, regarding it as a tool of the devil, now America became the inspiration for a revolution in social dancing which spread around the world.

Early in the century, the tango opened the door to such South American dances as the *rhumba* and *habanera,* all varying these rhythmic figures:

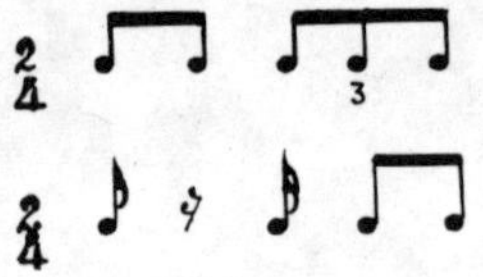

Tango rhythms (also used later in the samba)

Also later samba rhythms:

As American cities grew, people moved from large homes into apartments and hotels. To find places to dance, it became stylish to go to public halls, hotels, and, eventually, even churches opened the doors of their parish houses for youth dances. Soon dance floors became so crowded that it became difficult to dance the waltz and other dances demanding a spacious sweep, so new styles of dancing appeared with close embraces and up and down movements. These motions were introduced by a group of animal dances—the *turkey trot, bunny hug, lame duck, kangaroo hop,* and especially the *fox trot.*

Many features of the new dances were adopted from the African, who brought the rhythmic ecstasy and ritualistic emotions with him to America. Rhythm rippled through the limbs of many Blacks and into all the instruments they touched. In their dancing, they stamped their feet, clapped their hands, and shouted in joy.

The Cake Walk as Practised in Its Native Home

Ragtime was the first reflection of this when it appeared in New Orleans, bearing the rhythm of "Turkey in the Straw" and "Old Zip Coon":

"Old Zip Coon"

(This is the rhythm of "Downtown Rag," by Frank Signorelli and George Scarrozza, or of "Kitten on the Keys.) It quickly swept to Europe where Debussy wrote, "Le Petit Nigar," the "Golliwogs' Cakewalk" and "Général Lavine, Eccentrique"; Stravinsky wrote a piano rag, and Ravel wrote a charming fox trot.

Ragtime rhythm

Between 1910 and 1920, ragtime slowly became jazz. This was heralded by the exciting rhythmic combinations of the fox trot, in which the hopping movements of the dance were accompanied by accents on the second and fourth beats, which were often intensified by extra chords (chatterbox rag). Jazz also contained other rhythmic devices such as a three-note phrase embedded in 4/4 meter,

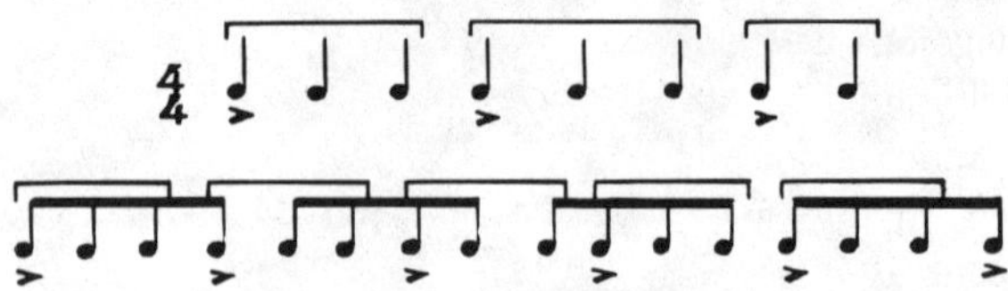

Polyrhythm of jazz

which Gershwin used in his "Rhapsody in Blue." (This is also exemplified in the popular song "I Can't Give You Anything but Love, Baby," by Dorothy Fields and Jimmy McHugh.)

To these devices, the blues added alterations in the scale, wherein melodic minor tones were used in major keys by lowering the third and seventh scale steps. Leonard Bernstein asserts that these blue notes were actually quarter-tones, representing the sound of the untrained human voice, slightly off key.

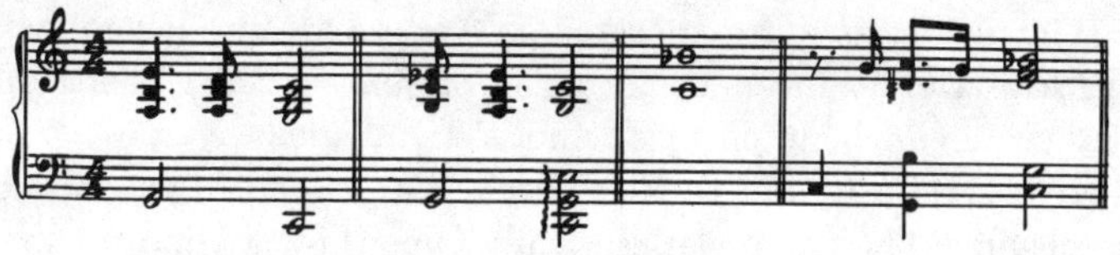

Blues progressions

These sounds were admirably suited to the wailing of the saxophone.

Of course, no written music can reveal the actual sounds of ragtime and jazz, which depended on improvisation wherein every performer added his own version of the tune and syncopation.

Social dancing also reflected the urge for individual freedom, and the primitive excitement of this new music heightened the emotions of the dancers. With jazz, the prescribed rules and regulations of dancing masters were cast aside, and people drifted with the music in whatever steps they felt suited their mood. Improvisation was again the order of the day. The dancers moved from side to side, swirled about, jiggled up and down on their toes, or merely walked back and forth.

Jazz and Tap

The vigorous new artistic era which appeared after World War I was highlighted by the influence of America and especially by the appearance of jazz. Europe was also spurred by the impact of the new rhythms and strident harmonies of Stravinsky's ballets and Schoenberg's atonal compositions. Indeed the Russian ballet with its promotion of the new primitivism of Stravinsky's works and the scenery of Picasso, Bakst, and others can be held responsible for much of the new art. When the armistice created a new era of prosperity, the jubilant Western world was swept by a wave of artistic freedom.

A search for new materials led to the creation of new artistic devices and the abandonment of many rules and theories. Americans became interested in the arts and, along with this, sought examples of purely American music and dance. Some found this with the Indians, some with the cowboys, and others with the Negroes. Many found it in jazz.

The word jazz first appeared in New Orleans, where reports began to refer to the unusual music played by Black bands. Most tales centered about one café much frequented by stage people, where a certain four-piece Black orchestra was noted for its eccentric playing. The group was especially famous for a blind trombonist who customarily added many improvisations and glissandos. When asked what he was playing, the trombonist replied, "Oh, I dunno—jus' jazz." It was also noted that none of the players could read music.

This band was brought to Chicago in about 1915, where it was billed under the name of its leader, the trombonist Tom Brown. It is reported that, when people first heard the band, they did not know what to make of the music. Finally the hotel manager stepped to the dance floor to explain that the music was intended for dancing. Only then did couples venture to dance, but, after a short time, the novelty became established and the music made the hotel so popular that crowds were turned away nightly. The new music soon spread to New York and all over the country. Europeans heard of the new sensation and soon invited jazz orchestras abroad.

This new music soon was adopted by composers of art music. Aaron Copland wrote a jazz piano concerto; Antheil wrote a jazz symphony and, in his *Ballet Mécanique* fused jazz with the music of machinery. These are a few among many.

Among the types of dancing performed to popular music, tap dancing was perhaps the most popular form of exhibition dance. The *tap dance* grew up and remained separate from ballet and art dancing; yet its highly spectacular nature developed a really artistic style of acrobatic dance notable for the manner with which the metallic shoes of the dancers emphasized the rhythm of music. Indeed, the dancers performed as a sort of percussion instrument, improvising a highly individual rhythmic accompaniment. Often they danced only to the sounds of their own feet.

Tap dancing was not an entirely new form of the dance. The old Lancashire clog, performed with wooden shoes, also relied on the sounds of feet. Indeed, among the first professional dancers in the United States were Irish clog dancers, wearing wooden-soled shoes. This Lancashire clog was adapted into the song and dance of the minstrel days. And, by eliminating the wooden shoes, this became known as the soft-shoe dance. It is said that, through this, the Negro of the minstrel show entered the picture of tap dancing. However other observers assert that the ancestor of tap was the "buck and wing" which included a mixture of clogs, jigs, song, and dance with other acrobatics.

In the early twentieth century, vaudeville dancers combined the Irish jig with the clog dance and then adapted them to jazz. Individual variations were added, some from Spain, but many from Negro sources. However, many dancers said they had developed their own style of tap dancing. Included among these was Bill Robinson, the great Negro tap dancer, who said he never had a lesson in his life and never imitated anyone, for as a child he developed his style of dancing on the streets of Richmond, Virginia.

The tap dance eventually developed until it used the entire body and its own characteristic style of motion, in which the rhythm of the music was accentuated by the sounds of the shoes which are shod at heel and toe with metal plates.

The speed with which dance music and its accompanying song spread was largely due to the commercialism of popular music. By the end of World War I, composers and publishers had ceased to rely on chance inspiration and customers. Vast corporations hired composers to write new tunes, which were sold by organizations which flooded the country with sheets of popular ballads. A host of devices increased the sales of the tunes by the use of musical shows, moving pictures, the phonograph, radio, and, later, television. In this manner the entire country was quickly alerted to all the new songs and lyrics of the day. And today we continue in the same manner.

Since the end of the Second World War in 1945, social dance music has not developed into art music for several reasons. Art music has grown steadily more abstract and complex. Following the scientific trends of the period, composers have sought new means of expression, new sounds, new forms, new theory, new instrumental combinations in twelve-tone serial composition, in electronic music and in other idioms. Each composer has desired to be new, intellectual, unique.

On the other hand, the social dance and its music have become steadily more primitive. Although dance floors continued to echo the popular tunes of jazz, swing and such, new elements were creeping in. The younger dancers performed as in primitive rites, largely bound together by the repeated drumming of a bass accompaniment in a series of variously named styles, such as *boogie,* followed by *rock and roll,* with its persistent ground bass, hard rock, acid rock, and others. Both the dancing and its music have turned more completely to improvisation. In their urge for freedom of motion and individualism, dancers gyrate in no set pattern of motion; often they move apart from their partners, who can oscillate in imitation, or do as they please in time to the beat. The guitar became one of the chief instruments of the era. It is simple to learn, and the player can strum a simple chord pattern in accompaniment to songs of folklike nature—often improvised, often played by ear. At the same time, electronic instruments and electronic amplification have taken over the sound, so that it is not so much the substance of the music, as the overwhelming mind-numbing rhythmic cacophony which intoxicates the dancer.

The Spectacular Dance

Meanwhile the theatrical dance began to change and now Russia began to unveil the progress of her ballet schools. In 1909, the new vigor of the Russian ballet under Serge Diaghilev was first revealed in Paris and created a sensation. While in Paris, Diaghilev discovered his countryman Stravinsky and forthwith invited him to compose the music of *The Firebird* for the choreographer Fokine. This was presented in 1910 and spurred greater changes in dancing, which were furthered upon the presentation of Stravinsky's next masterpiece, *Petrushka,* in 1911. The plot relates the strange tragedy of a puppet brought to life by a magician. The hysterical gaiety of the music with its new rhythms and strident harmonies proved the existence of a great new master of spectacular dance music. From then on, every new work of Stravinsky intensified the changes of the arts of music and the dance.

With the war, the Russian ballet had to leave Russia and moved to France and Monaco. Here a host of youthful artists and composers were commissioned by Diaghilev to work on ballets. This made the dance a truly great inspiration and the means of introducing many composers to the world.

While the Russian ballet was developing, the old-fashioned ballet was being challenged by other youthful innovators for its lack of realism. Tiring of the endless fairy-tale plots, the filmy costumes, and dancing slippers, dancers evolved a new form of the dance. Isadora Duncan was the first to appear. Wearing a simple Grecian tunic, she improvised her dancing to music of Chopin, Beethoven, and Bach, declaring she believed in a return to the simplicity of Grecian ideals.

Ruth St. Denis was a contemporary of Isadora Duncan and had great influence in the development of the new dance by breaking from the fetters of the conventional ballet and forming her own independent company. Yet, whereas Isadora's inspiration came from Greece, St. Denis derived hers from the Orient, and she adapted her dances from this source, although they were not really Oriental. Music was a great stimulus for her, and she not only followed the patterns of phrase and rhythm, but the emotional quality as well. Miss St. Denis gained added strength through her partner, Ted Shawn.

Ted Shawn was a strong force in the new dance. Yet, one of his strongest influences resulted from his successful effort to dispel the antipathy toward male dancing. Thus, in order to form a male dance corps, he recruited a group of athletes. These men were astounded at the rigorous training needed to produce a dancer and enthusiastically applied themselves in the new venture.

At the opposite pole, the Swiss musician Jacques Dalcroze devised a series of steps and body motions adapted for musical rhythms and phrases, to assist in understanding the basic structure of music. In 1913, the heads of the new Russian ballet, Diaghilev and Nijinsky asked Dalcroze to help them reinvigorate the ballet. Dalcroze sent Marie Rambert to Monte Carlo to teach the Russians. Her ideas so inspired Nijinsky that he applied them to his choreography of Stravinsky's *Rites of Spring,* which shocked the world with its brutality.

The *Rites of Spring* depicts pre-Christian pagan rites and the sacrifice of a consecrated virgin forced to dance until she dies from exhaustion. When first performed in Paris in 1913, both the music and Nijinsky's choreography shocked the audience, which was astounded to see dancers thudding barefoot on the stage. The audience created such an uproar that Diaghilev was compelled to stand up in his box and beg for silence. By the second act the tumult became so deafening that the tearful dancers could hardly hear the music. Then Marie Piltz began the dance of the consecrated virgin. Calmly facing the jeering audience with knees turned inwards and heels out, in anything but typical ballet form, she seemed suddenly shaken out of a trance by a spasm, and, trembling with ecstatic jerks, seemed swept by a primitive hysteria under the compelling force of the barbaric rhythms. Her superb interpretation overwhelmed the rebellious audience. Thus a new approach to the ballet was created.

The combination of all these factors culminated after the war, when new dance forms appeared. Marie Rambert went to London and there influenced Anthony Tudor and Frederick Ashton. Another disciple of Dalcroze, Mary Wigman, developed new forms of the expressional dance. Resenting Dalcroze's overemphasis on music, she preferred the absolute dance, basing her theories on the teaching of von Laban, who carefully analyzed the human body and motion. These were eventually incorporated into the von Laban system of dance notation.

Wigman's fame as a dancer spread to America and became a factor in developing a new type of spectacular dance later incorporated into "modern dance" by the famous dancers Martha Graham, Doris Humphrey, Charles Weidman, and Hanya Holm. Furthermore, Wigman's choice of percussive instruments for dance accompaniments became widely adopted.

Now, with the groundwork completed by 1920, the dance was ready for a new period, plus the possibility of interesting a vast public of viewers and promoting a host of young composers.

Twentieth-century dance has followed the scientific trends of the era. It has sought to discover the principles of human muscles in relation to motion and music. It has formulated new artistic forms.

Since this book is devoted to the music of the dance, we will list and illustrate the three, or really four, principle methods of securing music for the art:

1. a dance can be adapted to existing music;
2. a dance can be created to specially commissioned music;
3. music can be composed to already arranged dances;
4. purely percussive accompaniment can provide a rhythmic background. Likewise, an electronic background may be used.

Ballet depends almost entirely on the first two methods, and they have produced many masterpieces. However, many modern dancers have felt that music is a despotic master which tends to enslave the dance to its moods and rhythms. Others have argued that music is too intangible to enslave a choreographer, saying music evokes different associations and reactions in each person. Thus it stimulates the imagination differently; furthermore, music's rhythms make it a cohesive agent and a means of securing group unity. In addition, the emotional character of music makes it an important bridge between the thoughts of the dancer and the feelings of the audience.

Since 1910 our art music has been drastically changed. Composers have developed entirely different idioms. The harmonies and scales which were the basis of the music of the past have been rejected. New forms have been created. However, this music is singularly and often intentionally adapted to the needs of the dance. It is rhythmic, percussive, and even impersonal, lacking the sentimentality of the Romantic era and the vague harmonies and rhythms of the impressionists. Furthermore since the dance has become so popular, it has created an entirely new audience, requiring an entirely new musical idiom. Thus, where the nineteenth century favored the opera, the twentieth century favored the dance, and new composers quickly turned to dancers for their commissions, finding their livelihood therein.

In the 1920s, angular dance movement came into great prominence. This was a period of abstractionism and the dehumanized dance on an empty stage became typical; the dancer's face also became impersonal, and dancers even wore masks. At the same time, the emphasis on mere sex seems to have faded. It is probable that, after women adopted formfitting bathing suits, short skirts, and more revealing clothing, the interest in viewing feminine legs and figures on the stage became less important. Thus the dance developed a new type of visual appeal in which story, color, movement, and other spectacular elements took over. New treatments for masses of dancers also developed. Often it was attempted to carry over the lines and planes of cubistic and abstractionist paintings.

The male dancer also assumed increasing prominence. After audiences observed the prowess and virility of Nijinsky, the nineteenth-century stigma of effeminacy that had been attached to masculine dancing began to fade. Diaghilev lavished great favor upon his young men, and their leaps and acrobatics impressed the public.

The thirties saw the development of the expressional dance, spearheaded by the personalities of Martha Graham, Doris Humphrey, Charles Weidman, and Hanya Holm. They were very active in creating new dance idioms which are still called "modern dance." They performed barefoot; toe dancing was out, as well as the graceful poses and ballet technique of the past. A new technique was devised. The body was viewed as a "mirror of thought" for "the expression of inner compulsion." Martha Graham thought out the contraction-release principles of breathing. It was all new.

These dancers were keenly alive to their musical needs. Sometimes they tried unorthodox musical backgrounds such as gongs, a variety of drums, drinking glasses set to pitch, various vocal sounds. Doris Humphrey also turned to the music of the masters, and created a purely abstract dance to Bach's organ "Passacaglia in C minor." It is interesting for a spectator to observe that these dancers were not necessarily following the rhythms, phrases, and accents of the music, and might even be dancing against it or in spite of it.

In the creation of the music, if the composer was called in after the dancer had completely worked out the choreography, with every beat and step planned and mathematically measured, he was requested to write a score which would parallel every movement of the dancer. To write such music is a creative and technical feat of great merit. It is perhaps more difficult than the task of writing music with a stopwatch for the movies and television, although this technique became possible when dancers could film their dances in advance.

However the modern dancer rarely presented a composer with a definite form in which the movements had rhythmic regularity, possibilities of phrase structure, and evolution toward a climax. The dances of the past were based on parallel phrases and rhythmic structure and founded on precise step movements. The modern dancer on the other hand might request five bars of 4/4 time, three bars of 3/4 time with an accent on the second beat, six bars of 5/4 time with a hold over the last note, sudden speeding or slowing of the tempo. Many dancers cannot even present their rhythms in decipherable form. This creates tremendous difficulty for a composer.

It is interesting that the twentieth-century composer and twentieth-century music have been able to carry out such commissions and that musical style has become so purely abstract that it can fit into such situations.

Among modern dancers, Martha Graham was outstanding for her collaboration with composers. The list included such men as Darius Milhaud, Paul Hindemith (*Herodiade*), Samuel Barber (*Serpent Heart*), William Schumann (*Night Journey*), Norman Dello Joio (*The Triumph of St. Joan*), and, of course, Aaron Copland, whose *Appalachian Spring* is regarded among our great masterpieces for both arts.

Meanwhile, other nations became interested in developing their own schools of dance. Denmark and Sweden saw the beginnings of notable groups. England saw the establishment of the Sadler's Wells Ballet in 1931 upon the initiative of the Dublin choreographer Ninette de Valois, who had danced with Diaghilev. A notable early work was her *Job,* based on music commissioned to Vaughn Williams. Sadler's Wells soon developed the great choreographers Anthony Tudor and Frederick Ashton. Ashton used such previously composed tone poems as Delius's "Paris" and Arnold Bax's "Garden of Fane," among others.

Eventually Anthony Tudor was invited to America when Diaghilev's former ballet company was reestablished. There he exerted great influence upon the development of American ballet. Tudor's particular contribution was the psychological ballet, which became prominent in the late thirties. His work was based upon the ballet technique he learned from Marie Rambert, but assayed a stream-of-consciousness method wherein the dancer interprets character upon psychological motivation. William Schumann's *Undertow* is an example of this principle. Tudor aroused considerable discussion for his use of music by refusing to be controlled by the formal details of the composition. Thus dancers might move rapidly to slow music and even stand still as an orchestra thundered to a climax.

Agnes De Mille is honored by being credited as the first American choreographer to use an American theme for a work of a major ballet company. This was Aaron Copland's *Rodeo,* presented in 1942 by the Ballet Russe de Monte Carlo. One of her most exciting works was the morbid psychological *Fall River Legend,* based on a score by Morton Gould. Another achievement of Miss De Mille was the musical *Oklahoma,* in which the psychological ballet entered the field of musical comedy.

We now reach the great Russian-born choreographer George Balanchine, whose influence upon American ballet has practically brought the actual renaissance of classical ballet. Educated in Russia as a concert pianist, as well as a finely trained ballet dancer, he left Russia after the First World War and joined with Diaghilev as a dancer. By 1925, he had begun to choreograph outstanding compositions. Following Diaghilev's death, he was invited to direct the School of American Ballet by Gerald Warburg and ballet's great patron, Lincoln Kirstein. After a brief and stormy association with the Metropolitan Opera House, Balanchine and his great patron and friend, Lincoln Kirstein, gradually developed the famous New York City Ballet, which was finally installed in a great new theater in New York's Lincoln Center.

Balanchine's predilection is the absolute classical dance, and his inspiration is music. He prefers specially commissioned music in which he can advise composers of his intentions for dance action. However with precomposed music, he thoroughly familiarizes himself with the intentions of the composer before outlining his action. Stravinsky preferred to work with Balanchine in many of his later works, and it is said that the great highlight of the 1948 season was the Stravinsky-Balanchine *Orpheus,* which is said to have been instrumental in the establishment of the New York City Ballet.

Before concluding our brief study of the dance, mention must be made of the recording of dance motion. Until recently, the art of music has been in a far more favorable position for study than the dance; for music has had a standard method of notation since the fifteenth century and has thereby tangibly preserved its literature. More recently, recordings have further preserved the authenticity of performance.

The dance has had no such record until the invention of the motion-picture camera. True, various systems of notation have existed since Feuillet and the early eighteenth century. Indeed we might go back to the more incomprehensible notation of the fifteenth-century basse dance. Yet, none of these systems has preserved the essence of style and movement, which, like dress fashions, has varied with each passing year, as observers of old motion pictures may attest. As a result, after a very few years, the most that has remained from the labor and artistry of a dance spectacle is a fond memory, except perhaps in literary memoirs and the music.

Since 1928, accurate dance notation has become possible through the effort of Rudolph Laban, a German engineer who published the *Labanotation* which bears his name. Since then, a few world specialists have managed to write out some hundred ballet scores. At the same time, Rudolph Benesh devised a method called choreology, which dominates British ballet. Both methods are excellent, but it required days of intense effort to write the choreography by hand, and only a few dancers have been able to read the script.

However, a typewriterlike instrument has been created by IBM which can be used to cut the hours, days, and weeks needed to record the choreography of a dance, and, with a new computerized method, great results are expected. This was demonstrated in October 1976 by Muriel Topaz, chief Laban notator of the Dance Notation Bureau. At the same time new methods for teaching the reading of dance notation have been developed. These will enable the dance to have a continuous documented history as well as cheaper and more authentic possibilities for reproducing an established repertory. Thus dance will enter a new era.

In conclusion, we observe that most great dancing since primitive times has been characterized by the unity of the arts of music and dance. Although dancing may be exciting to see and to experience, a spectator can only view motion with the eyes; his emotions can be reached more quickly through the catalytic agency of music, which, through its mood, can form an important bridge between the thought of the dancer and the mind of the viewer. The pioneers of the early motion pictures early discovered that music helped sustain interest and bridge action with its emotional content. Music, likewise, heightens the joy of watching dance movement.

In the future, the development of the combined arts depends on their interplay. New motion will suggest new music, and, conversely, new music will suggest new motion, and both arts will mirror the changing cultural concepts of man.

Bibliography

Comprehensive Histories of the Dance

Beaumont, Cyril. *Complete Book of Ballet.* New York: G. P. Putnam, 1938.

Bie, Oscar. *Tanzmusik von Oscar Vie.* Berlin: Bard, Marquarde, et al, 1905.

Compan, Charles. *Dictionnaire de la danse.* Paris: Cailleau, 1787.

Desrat, G. *Dictionnaire de la danse.* Paris: Libraires imprimaries réunis, 1895.

Fertiault, François. *Histoire anecdotique et pittoresque de la danse.* Paris: A. Aubry, 1854.

Kirsten, Lincoln. *Dance.* New York: G. P. Putnam, 1935.

Nettl, Paul. *The Story of Dance Music.* New York: Philosophical Library, 1947.

Sachs, Curt. *World History of the Dance.* New York: W. W. Norton, 1937, 1963.

Sharp, Cecil and Oppe. *The Dance: An Historical Survey.* London: H. & T. Smith, 1934.

Vuillier, Gaston. *A History of Dancing from Earliest Ages.* New York: D. Appleton, 1897.

Specialized Fields

Annuals of the Imperial Theatres, The. Russian, 1891-1915.

Arbeau, Thoinot. *Orchesography.* C. W. Beaumont, trans. London (also New York: Evans, Kamin Dance, 1948).

Amberg, George. *Ballet in America.* New York: Duell, Sloan and Pearce, 1949.

Aubry, Pierre. *Estampies et danses royales*. Paris: Fischbacher, 1897.

Bauer, Marion. *Twentieth Century Music*. New York: W. W. Norton, 1939.

Beaumont, Cyril. *Three French Dancers of the 18th Century*. London: C. W. Beaumont, 1934.

Blasis, Carlo. *The Code of Terpsichore*. R. Barton, trans. London: E. Bull, 1830.

Bukofzer, Manfred. *Music in the Baroque Era*. New York: W. W. Norton, 1947.

———. *Studies in Medieval and Renaissance Music*. New York: W. W. Norton, 1950.

Chase, Gilbert. *The Music of Spain*. New York: W. W. Norton, 1941.

Cohen, Helen L. *Lyric Forms from France*. New York: Harcourt Brace, 1922.

Copland, Aaron. *Copland on Music*. Garden City, New York: Doubleday, 1960.

Danckert, Werner. Geschichte der Gigue. Leipzig: F. Kistner and Co., 1924 (also W. Siegel, 1924).

Dolmetsche, Mabel. *Dances of England and France from* 1450-1600. London: Routledge & Kegan Paul, 1949.

Einstein, Alfred. "Die Aria di Ruggiero." *Sammelbande der Internationalen Musikgesellschaft,* XIII, 1911-12.

———. *Gluck*. London: J. M. Dent and Sons, Ltd., 1936.

Froissart, G. Coulton. *The Chronicler of European Chivalry*. London: The Studio, Ltd., 1930.

Gautier, Theophile. *The Romantic Ballet*. C. W. Beaumont, trans. London: C. W. Beaumont, 1932.

Gennrich, Friedrich. *Rondeaux, Virelais und Balladen aus dem Ende des XII den XIII Jahrhundert aus der Gesellschaft fur Rumanische Literature*. Gottingen, 1921, 1927.

Goldberg, Isaac. *Tin Pan Alley*. New York: The John Day Co., 1930.

Gombosi, Otto. "Dur Fruhgeschichte der Folia." *Acta Musicologica,* VIII, p. 119, 1937.

———. "Italia Patria del Basso Ostinato." *La Rassegna Musicale,* XIV, 1934.

———. Cultural and Folkloristic Background of the Folia. Papers of the American Musicological Society, 1940.

Imbert, De Saint-Amand, A. L. *Famous Women of the Valois Court*. New York: C. Scribner's Sons, 1892-93.

Ivanoff, N. "Les fêtes a la cour des derniers Valois." France: *Révue du seizième siècle,* v. 19, 1932.

Kinkeldey, Otto. *A Jewish Dancing Master of the Renaissance*. New York: Freidus Memorial Volume, 1929.

La Laurencie, Lionel. *Rameau*. Paris: H. Laurens, 1908.

Liszt, Franz. *Life of Chopin*. John Broadhouse, trans. London: W. Reeves, 1913.

Martin, John. *Introduction to the Dance*. New York: W. W. Norton, 1939.

———. Introduction to the Dance. New York: A. S. Barnes and Co., 1933.

Masson, Paul Marie. *L'opéra de Rameau*. Paris: H. Laurens, 1930 (Reprint New York: Da Capo Press, 1972).

Mellers, Wilfrid Howard. *François Couperin and the French Classical Tradition*. New York: Dover, 1968.

Moser, Andreas. "Folies d'Espagne." *Archiv fur Musikwissenschaft,* 1, 1919.

Nettl, Paul. "Zwei Spanische Ostinatothemen." *Zeitschrift fur Musikwissenschaft,* 1, 1919.

Nichols, J. *Progresses of Elizabeth*. London: J. Nichols, 1823.

Noverre, Jean George. *Lettres sur la danse et sur les ballets*. France: A. Delaroche, 1760.

Osgood, Henry O. *So This Is Jazz*. Boston: Little, Brown & Co., 1926.

Parry, Charles H. *Johann Sebastian Bach*. London: Putnam, 1934.

Perugini, Mark Edward. *The Pageant of the Dance and Ballet*. London: Jarrolds, Ltd., 1935.

Prunières, Henri. *Le ballet de cour en France avant Benserade et Lully*. Paris: A. Laurens, 1914 (Reprint New York: Johnson, 1970).

Pulver, Jeffrey. "The Gig." Proceedings of the Musical Association of England, Feb. 17, 1914, sessions 39 and 40.

Rameau, Pierre. *The Dancing Master*. Cyril Beaumont, trans. London: C. W. Beaumont, 1931 (Reprint New York: Dance Horizons, 1970).

Reese, Gustave. *Music in the Middle Ages*. New York: W. W. Norton, 1940.

Sachs, Curt. "Some Remarks about Old Notations." *Musical Quarterly,* vol. XXXIV, 3.

Sharp, Cecil J. *The Country Dance Book.* London: Novello & Co., 1909-16.

Solerti, Angelo. *Musica, Ballo e Dramatica alla Corte Medicea del 1600-1637.* Florence: R. Bemporad et Figlio, 1905.

Stravinsky, Igor. *An Autobiography.* New York: Simon and Schuster, 1936.

Tansman, Alexandre. *Igor Stravinsky.* New York: G. P. Putnam, 1949.

Welsford, Enid. *The Court Masque.* Cambridge, England: Cambridge University Press, 1927.

Whiteman, Paul. *Jazz.* New York: J. H. Sears and Co., Inc., 1926.

Index

See also Polacca